The Human Algorithm

Demystifying AI-Driven Hiring for Modern Talent Leaders

Verses Kindler Publication

Verses Kindler Publication.

Website: www.verseskindlerpublication.com

The Human Algorithm

Demystifying AI-Driven Hiring for Modern Talent Leaders

By: Dr. Sachin Shenoy

ISBN: 978-93-47494-78-9

1st Edition

Price: INR 399/$18

Disclaimer

The Human Algorithm :*Demystifying AI-Driven Hiring for Modern Talent Leaders* **is** authored by Dr. Sachin Shenoy. The entirety of this published work comprises the original content of the author, who has undertaken diligent efforts in its editing. The characters depicted herein may be fictitious or inspired by real events; however, they are not intended to cause offense or represent any prejudice against any caste or system. Any similarity to the names of actual individuals, locations, or institutions is purely coincidental and serves the narrative. The author bears sole responsibility for the originality of this work; the publisher assumes no liability thereof.

Contents

Author's Note

When I began my doctoral research on the impact of AI on talent acquisition in Indian IT and ITeS companies, most conversations about AI in hiring sat at two extremes: breathless optimism or nervous dismissal. Either AI was going to magically "fix" everything, or it was going to replace everyone.

The data and the lived stories of recruiters, leaders, and candidates told a different story.

Used well, AI can remove friction and expand the talent pool. More importantly, it gives recruiters the time to do deeply human work. Used badly, it can amplify noise, harden bias, and reduce people to scores they never see or understand.

This book sits in the necessary middle ground: optimistic about what is possible, honest about what can go wrong, and practical about what to do next.

You will not find vendor feature comparisons here. This book will also not make a promise that one tool will solve all your problems. Instead, you will find:

- Basic guidelines for understanding how AI can truly benefit hiring and where it shouldn't take charge.
- Concrete examples, visuals, and playbooks drawn from research and practice in IT and ITeS.
- Questions you can ask your teams, vendors, and yourself before switching anything on.

Although my research was rooted in India, the patterns I saw are now visible across markets: similar pressures, similar hopes, similar mistakes. My goal with this book is not to add to the noise. Instead, I wish to provide you with a common language and useful tools for creating effective AI-enabled hiring that works for your context.

If you are a recruiter, I hope these pages help you reclaim time and influence.
If you are a TA or business leader, I hope they help you invest with clarity instead of chasing hype.
And if you are a candidate, I hope it reassures you that many of us on the inside are trying to make the system worthy of your trust.

Thank you for taking this journey with me.

Dedication

They say it takes a village to raise a child. In my case, it took a global network to bring both a thesis and this book to life.

I am deeply grateful to Dr. Sara Pax, whose guidance during my doctoral journey helped shape the research behind this book. Her sharp feedback and steady support gave these pages their foundation.

My thanks also go to the experts who validated my research instruments and to the 600+ professionals who contributed their time and insights to my study on AI and talent acquisition. Your input turned questions into evidence and evidence into practical ideas.

Most of all, I dedicate this book to my wife and daughter, who stayed with me through every stage of this DBA journey. Your patience, humour, and belief kept me going.

Finally, this book is for the recruiters and candidates who live this process every day. Recruiters carry the unseen work behind every hire, and candidates carry the hope and uncertainty on the other side of it. You are the reason it matters that AI makes hiring not only faster, but also fairer and more human.

If this book were a film about the future of hiring, each of you would be in the opening credits. Thank you for being part of this journey.

1

The AI Talent Crunch in India's Tech Economy

Indian IT and ITeS companies have never had more opportunity than they do today. Digital transformation, cloud migration, AI, cybersecurity, and data engineering have made Indian tech talent central to global value chains. Yet the ability to find, assess, and hire the right people is now a strategic bottleneck, not a back-office function.

At exactly the same time, artificial intelligence has quietly moved from the margins of recruitment to its core. Applicant tracking systems are upgraded with AI screening. Chatbots answer candidate queries at midnight. Video interview platforms claim to read everything from competencies to culture fit. For many leaders, the hope is simple: use AI to hire faster and cheaper. The reality, however, is more complex.

India's Tech Engine and the New Hiring Squeeze

Over the last decade, India's IT and ITeS sectors have become pillars of the national economy. As per a report by NASSCOM, India's technology industry was estimated at $254 billion in

FY2024, with exports continuing to account for a major share of that value. This growth has been especially visible across Bengaluru, Hyderabad, Pune, Chennai, Delhi-NCR, and Mumbai, where IT services firms, product companies, GCCs, and large ITeS players compete for overlapping talent pools.

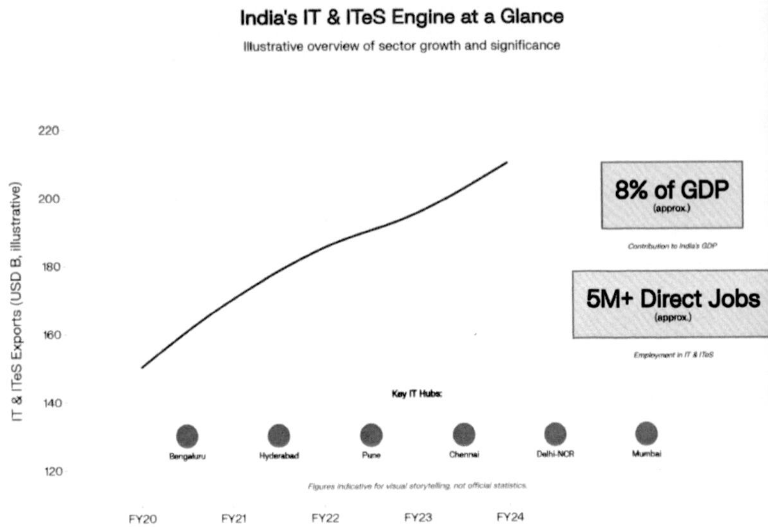

As a result, the nature of hiring has changed. In an industry employing millions and supporting more than 1,700 GCCs in India alone, talent acquisition is no longer just about filling roles. It is about orchestrating capacity for complex, multi-country projects under tight timelines. Project start dates and service agreements often depend on how quickly teams can hire for key roles like cloud, AI/ML, cybersecurity, full-stack engineering, data science, business analysis, and specialized operations. What was once a human resources problem is now a core business continuity risk. A recruiter in Bengaluru described reviewing over 500 resumes for a single role under tight deadlines. "You stop reading properly after a point," she said. "You're just trying to keep up." This is the environment in which AI is being introduced.

In this environment, three forces make talent acquisition uniquely challenging:

- **Volume:** Large IT and ITeS firms routinely handle thousands of applications and hundreds of open requisitions at any point in time.
- **Velocity:** Client commitments and quarterly business pressures demand rapid ramp-ups, often with little notice for TA teams.
- **Variability:** The mix ranges from high-volume customer support roles to hyper-specialized architects and product leaders, each requiring very different assessment strategies.

Traditional recruitment models, manual shortlisting, loosely structured interviews, and spreadsheet-based tracking were not designed for this level of volume, velocity, and variability. As one recruitment manager from our study put it, "We are trying to fight modern fires with vintage hoses."

From Resumes to Algorithms: How Hiring Has Already Changed

To cope, many organizations have progressively digitized their recruitment processes. Job postings are syndicated via career sites and portals. Candidate data flows into applicant tracking systems. Background checks are integrated through APIs.

In the last five years, this digitization has accelerated into automation and AI:

- **AI-enabled resume screening** ranks candidates against job descriptions, sometimes within minutes.
- **Chatbots and virtual assistants** answer FAQs, schedule interviews, and nudge candidates to complete assessments.
- **Video interviewing platforms** use structured question banks and, in some implementations elsewhere, analytics on speech and behaviour.
- **Predictive models** attempt to forecast candidate success or the likelihood of accepting offers, enabling more targeted follow-up.

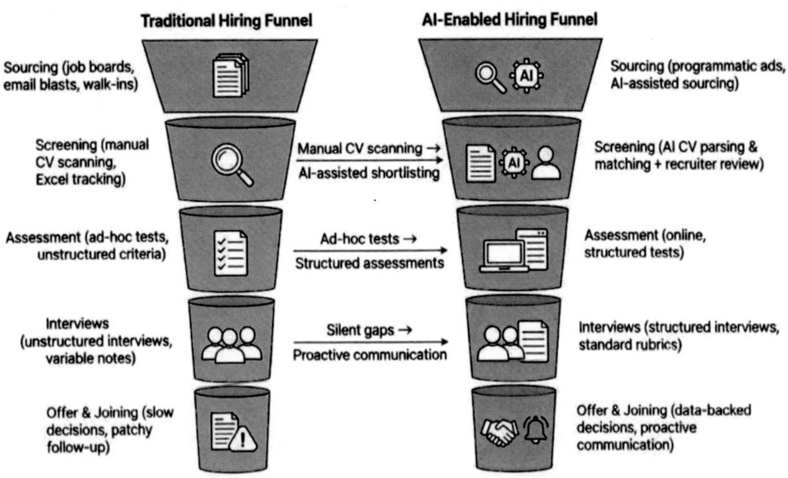

Comparison of a traditional recruitment funnel and an AI-enabled recruitment funnel in IT and ITeS.

Our research found that a substantial proportion of IT and ITeS organizations in India already employ at least one AI-enabled tool in their hiring process, whether in sourcing, screening, or communication. However, adoption is uneven: large, well-resourced ITeS organizations tend to deploy more advanced and integrated solutions, while many mid-sized IT firms use AI features in a piecemeal fashion through job portals or basic ATS add-ons.

This uneven adoption is important because it directly influences the impact organizations see. The same technology, when deployed as an isolated widget versus as part of a redesigned process, produces very different outcomes, a theme we will revisit throughout this book.

Why Traditional Talent Acquisition Is Breaking

Even without AI, Indian TA teams have been under strain for years. Studies and industry reports have highlighted persistent pain points: weak employer branding in certain segments, uneven sourcing pipelines, and high early attrition in some roles. Our research and review of the literature confirm several structural issues that traditional methods struggle to overcome:

1. **Manual, error-prone screening**
   Recruiters often wade through large volumes of resumes, making rapid, heuristic decisions under time pressure. This leads to inconsistent shortlisting, missed fits, and fatigue.

2. **Fragmented processes and tools**
   Job boards, email, spreadsheets, ATS, and assessment portals rarely form a seamless workflow. Information is

duplicated, lost, or delayed, slowing time-to-hire and frustrating stakeholders.

3. **Limited visibility and analytics**
   While "time-to-fill" and "offer-to-join" are tracked, granular visibility into each stage, such as where drop-offs occur or which sourcing channels truly deliver quality hires, is often missing.

4. **Inconsistent candidate experience**
   Candidates frequently report silence after applying, vague communication about stages, and little feedback after rejection. These are issues that damage an employer's brand and reduce the likelihood of receiving applications in the future.

5. **Strain on recruiters**
   High requisition loads force recruiters to prioritize

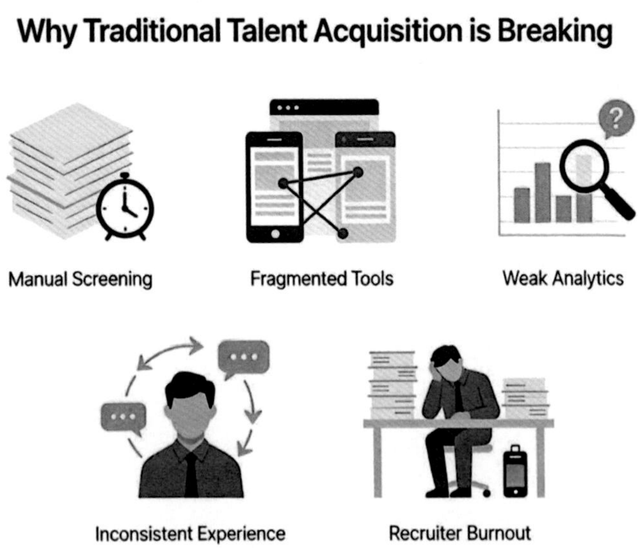

speed over depth, relying on shortcuts and gut feel. This increases the risk of mis-hire and intensifies burnout.

In such a context, it is understandable that AI is seen as a potential savior: a way to restore order to unmanageable volume and speed. But technology introduced on top of broken processes has a tendency to amplify underlying weaknesses instead of solving them.

The Promise of AI, And What the Data Actually Shows

Before this study, most claims about AI-enabled recruitment in India came from vendor marketing, isolated case studies, or global research applied loosely to the Indian context. There was limited independent evidence linking AI use to concrete outcomes such as time-to-hire, cost-per-hire, recruiter efficiency, candidate experience, and perceived fairness across both IT and ITeS sectors.

This research helps close that gap. Our quantitative survey of 286 recruitment professionals and 270 candidates across IT and ITeS organizations reveals several important patterns:

- **AI-enabled recruitment tools are significantly associated with reductions in time-to-hire and cost-per-hire**, with the effect being stronger in ITeS organizations than in IT firms.
- **Structured automation in resume screening and shortlisting improves operational efficiency**, with a regression coefficient of 0.62, statistically significant at the 0.01 level.

- **Candidate experience improves meaningfully only when AI-driven processes are combined with high-quality communication,** timely updates, clarity on stages, and feedback, because communication quality mediates the relationship between technology use and candidate experience (coefficient 0.48, $p < 0.05$).
- **Both professionals and candidates tend to perceive AI tools as largely fair and unbiased,** although the underlying mechanisms of fairness are rarely examined systematically.

In short, AI, when thoughtfully implemented, can genuinely help organizations hire faster and at lower cost. But the data also shows that efficiency is not the same as experience, and that the benefits are not automatic. They depend heavily on how tools are integrated into processes and how human interaction is preserved and enhanced.

The Real Risks of Getting AI-Enabled Recruitment Wrong

While the upside is significant, the risks of poorly designed AI-enabled recruitment are just as real. These risks fall into three broad categories.

Operational and Financial Risk

If AI tools are introduced without redesigning workflows, they can add complexity rather than reduce it. Recruiters may have to reconcile outputs from multiple systems, candidates may be forced through redundant steps, and hiring managers may receive information they do not know how to interpret.

In our study, professionals who reported fragmented tool ecosystems also reported more frequent bottlenecks, even when AI features were present. The result is paradoxical: investment in AI without corresponding gains in speed or quality, leading stakeholders to question the value of the transformation.

Reputational and Experience Risk

From a candidate's perspective, automation without communication feels cold and opaque. Candidates in our sample expressed greater trust and satisfaction when digital systems provided clear, timely information about their status and next steps. When this is absent, AI-based processes are perceived as impersonal "black boxes," and candidates are more likely to share negative experiences on social media and professional networks.

For IT and ITeS firms competing not just on compensation but also on brand and career promise, a reputation for indifferent, automated hiring can quietly erode their ability to attract top talent.

Ethical and Regulatory Risk

Globally, concerns about algorithmic bias, transparency, and data privacy are increasingly being reflected in emerging regulatory frameworks and industry guidance. AI systems trained on historical hiring data can inadvertently reproduce past discrimination, even if current practitioners believe they are neutral.

In our study, both professionals and candidates tended to view AI tools as generally fair, but very few organizations had formal processes to audit AI outputs or explain decisions to stakeholders. This gap between perceived fairness and actual governance is a risk waiting to materialize, especially in a diverse, stratified labour market like India's, where biases related to gender, institution tier, geography, and language can easily be encoded into data.

As AI regulation evolves, organizations will need to demonstrate not only that they use AI, but that they use it responsibly.

The Leadership Decision Point: Patch, Buy, or Redesign?

Many CHROs and TA heads today find themselves at a crossroads with three broad options:

1. **Patch the existing system**
   Continue with primarily manual processes, making incremental improvements and minor automation where possible.

2. **Buy more tools**
   Invest in additional AI-enabled solutions, new screening tools, more sophisticated assessments, and smarter chatbots, without fundamentally rethinking process design or governance.

3. **Redesign the hiring model around AI and humans working together.**
   Step back and reimagine the entire talent acquisition funnel, defining where AI can reliably add speed and consistency, where human judgment is essential, and

how communication and fairness will be protected end-to-end.

The evidence from this study suggests that the third option is

the only sustainable path. AI works best not as a layer pasted on top of legacy processes, but as part of a deliberately designed system in which:

- Automation handles high-volume, rules-based work such as initial screening, routine communication, and scheduling.
- Humans focus on high-value activities: understanding nuanced role requirements, assessing complex fit, influencing stakeholders, and building relationships with candidates.
- Processes are continuously monitored for efficiency, experience, and fairness, using clear metrics and feedback loops.

This book is a guide to help leaders make that shift. It translates empirical evidence from Indian IT and ITeS organizations into frameworks, tools, and playbooks that can be implemented in real-world settings, under real constraints.

How to Read This Book

Each of the following chapters builds on the foundation laid here:

- **Chapter 2** dissects why many AI-enabled recruitment initiatives under-deliver, even in sophisticated organizations.
- **Chapter 3** explains the research in more depth, summarizing what 556 professionals and candidates revealed about AI, efficiency, experience, and fairness.
- **Chapter 4** shows how to design an AI-first, human-centred hiring funnel in practice.
- **Chapter 5** provides an actionable framework for building fair and transparent AI in recruitment.
- **Chapter 6** focuses on transforming recruiters into AI-powered talent partners.
- **Chapter 7** dives into designing candidate experiences that are both digital-first and deeply human.
- **Chapter 8** offers sector-specific playbooks and a 180-day roadmap for leaders who want to move from scattered pilots to scaled, governed AI in talent acquisition.

You do not need a background in statistics or data science to use this book. Where we reference findings such as regression coefficients or mediation effects, we will translate them into simple, practical implications: what to do more of, what to stop, and what to redesign.

The core message of this chapter, and of the book, is straightforward: AI in recruitment is neither a magic bullet nor a passing fad. It is a powerful set of tools that, when combined with thoughtful process design and human judgment, can help Indian IT and ITeS organizations hire faster, fairer, and smarter. The leaders who act on this now will not just win the next hiring cycle; they will shape the future of work in one of the world's most important technology ecosystems.

2

Unlocking the Full Potential of AI-Enabled Recruitment: What's Holding You Back?

Most leaders who invest in AI for recruitment do it with clear expectations: fewer manual tasks, faster hiring, better matches, and a slicker candidate experience. Yet when you talk to TA heads across Indian IT and ITeS organizations, a different story emerges: partial gains, uneven adoption, and a nagging feeling that the return on investment does not match the promise.

This chapter explains why, drawing on patterns surfaced in both the existing literature and the 556 professionals and candidates who participated in the research behind this book. It shows that the problem is rarely the algorithm alone. The real issues lie in **how** AI is bolted onto legacy processes, **what** organizations communicate (or fail to communicate) to candidates, and **where** humans are pushed out of the loop.

The Tool Trap: Why Buying AI Does Not Fix Hiring

Over the past few years, the Indian HR and TA ecosystem has seen an explosion of AI-enabled products: smart ATS platforms, AI resume parsers, sourcing engines, chatbots, video interview tools, and predictive analytics dashboards. Many IT and ITeS organizations responded by adding AI features to existing tech stacks in the hope that automation would fix long-standing bottlenecks in sourcing, screening, and coordination.

The research record shows a similar pattern. Studies from Indian IT contexts describe AI tools reducing manual screening, assisting with vacancy prediction, and improving recruiter productivity. At the same time, those same studies repeatedly acknowledge small samples, narrow geographies, or limited sectors, Pune-based IT firms, Chennai IT employees, Delhi-NCR SMEs and startups, which makes it difficult to generalize claims or translate them into robust, organization-wide playbooks.

In practice, several failure modes appear:

- **AI as a widget, not a system.** Tools are introduced as add-ons to existing workflows instead of triggering a redesign of the end-to-end hiring process. Recruiters

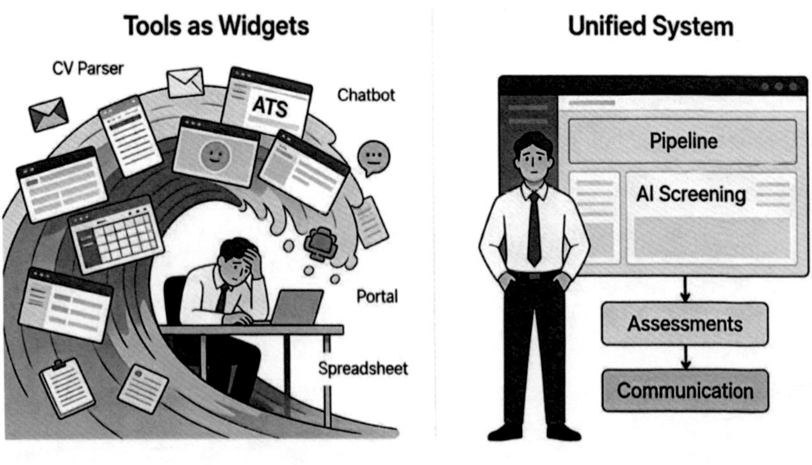

now check one more dashboard, export one more spreadsheet, or reconcile one more set of scores.

- **Unclear ownership.** No one is explicitly accountable for model inputs, parameter choices, or periodic reviews; responsibility is assumed to sit somewhere between vendor, IT, HR, and legal.
- **Shallow success metrics.** Adoption is celebrated when logins go up, or screens look modern, even though core indicators like time-to-hire, cost-per-hire, or candidate experience barely improve.

Our survey data confirms this misalignment. Professionals widely associate AI with improved productivity and faster screening, yet there are pockets of neutral or negative responses where users experienced complexity rather than simplification. When tools are layered onto unchanged processes, recruiters may end up working **for** the system instead of the system working for them.

Case in Point: Digital Hiring at Scale at TCS

TCS has built one of the largest digital hiring engines in India, combining online testing, automated workflows, and integrated platforms to manage large candidate volumes. The success of this approach comes not from isolated tools, but from aligning process design, communication, and evaluation methods.

This reinforces a key point from this chapter: organisations that treat AI as part of an end-to-end system see more consistent outcomes than those that simply layer tools onto existing processes.

Identifying the Cracks in the Candidate Experience

If internal users feel the friction, candidates feel it even more. They interact with AI indirectly, via portals, auto-generated emails, assessments, or chatbots, but what they remember is whether the process felt clear, respectful, and worth their time.

The study provides two critical insights:

1. **Candidates report higher trust, transparency, and satisfaction when digital recruitment systems provide prompt communication and feedback.**
2. **Communication quality significantly mediates the relationship between technology usage and candidate experience, with a mediation coefficient of 0.48 ($p < 0.05$).**

So, AI alone does not improve experience. AI plus good communication does. Where organizations fall short is that they treat communication as a "nice-to-have," rather than acknowledging it as a core design parameter.

Typical breakpoints include:

- **After application:** Candidates submit profiles to AI-driven systems but receive no acknowledgement beyond a generic email.
- **After AI-based screening or tests:** They complete online assessments or asynchronous video responses, then enter a "silent zone" with no visibility into outcomes.

- **After rejection:** Standardized, non-specific rejection emails leave candidates guessing whether the decision came from a human, an algorithm, or both.

Where the Candidate Journey Breaks

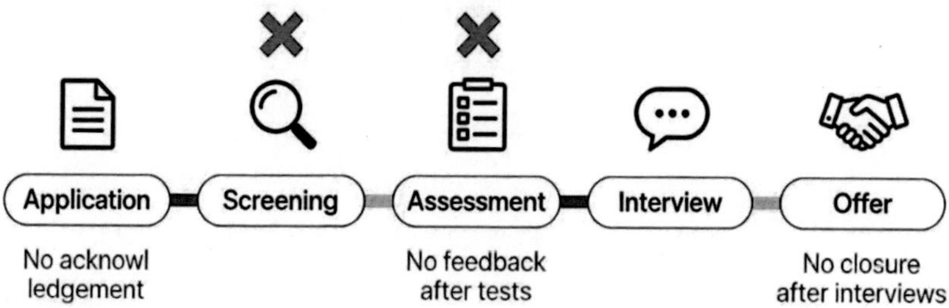

The data shows that when candidates know AI is used but are not told **how** or **why**, their satisfaction drops, even if the underlying algorithms are technically sound. Conversely, when organizations clearly explain the process and provide timely status updates, candidate experience scores rise, even in heavily automated hiring flows.

For Indian IT and ITeS firms competing in a market where skilled professionals often juggle multiple offers, this is not a cosmetic issue. It is a strategic vulnerability. Poorly communicated AI processes can push top talent toward competitors who appear more transparent and human, even if they use similar tools behind the scenes.

The Illusion of Fairness: Why Trust Can Be Misleading

A striking finding from the study is how **positive** both professionals and candidates are about AI fairness, at least on the surface. Descriptive analysis for fairness-related items shows mean scores above 6 on a 7-point scale for many statements indicating that AI tools evaluate candidates impartially and fairly.

At the same time, there is nuance:

- Some respondents strongly agree that AI tools should be monitored for bias and fairness, with candidates slightly more insistent on continuous oversight than professionals.
- ANOVA results show that perceptions of bias risk vary across experience levels, with more seasoned participants more likely to question whether AI may disadvantage underrepresented groups.

This produces an "illusion of fairness" effect. Because AI is perceived as mathematical and objective, it is often assumed to be neutral by default. But the literature and broader global experience act as a cautionary counterweight: AI algorithms trained on historical hiring data can encode gender, institution-tier, geography, or language biases unless they are explicitly checked and corrected.

The current state in many organizations looks like this:

- **High trust, low auditing.** People believe AI is fair but rarely test this belief via systematic fairness reviews.

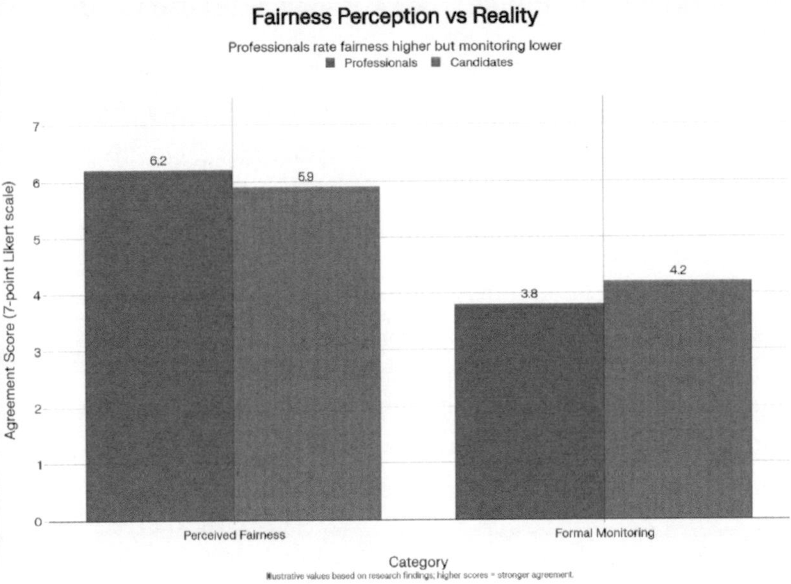

- **Positive experiences, limited awareness.** Candidates who personally feel treated fairly may still be aware, in the abstract, that these systems can disadvantage others, especially underrepresented groups.
- **Ethical frameworks on paper, not in practice.** While several conceptual models propose accountability, responsibility, and transparency principles, empirical evidence of consistent application in Indian IT and ITeS recruitment is scarce.

The danger is clear: **perceived fairness can delay the urgency to build real fairness controls.** By the time issues surface publicly, through legal complaints or viral social posts, the damage to trust and brand can be hard to reverse.

From Promise to Pitfall: Four Missteps in AI-Enabled Recruitment

Putting the data and literature together, four recurring failure patterns emerge across organizations experimenting with AI-enabled recruitment.

1. Over-Automation of Critical Touchpoints

In the pursuit of speed, some organizations allow AI systems to dominate early and mid-journey decisions without sufficient human review, particularly in high-volume roles. Candidates interact mainly with portals, emails, and bots, and only meet a human recruiter late in the process, if at all.

This saves time but carries three risks: missing non-obvious talent, failing to assess context-specific fit, and eroding candidate trust in the process.

2. Under-Investment in Communication

The mediation analysis in the study is unambiguous: communication quality is a powerful lever. Yet many AI projects are scoped as "tool deployments," with little budget or attention devoted to designing communication templates, candidate FAQs, or status dashboards.

The result is a highly automated engine wrapped in a thin layer of generic, reactive communication, which is exactly the opposite of what candidates say they want.

3. No Structured Monitoring of Bias or Performance

While organizations measure basic KPIs like time-to-hire and stage-wise conversion, very few routinely examine:

- Shortlist and offer rates by gender, geography, or institution category.
- Whether certain groups are more likely to be filtered out at the AI screening stage versus later human stages.
- Whether models drift over time as job requirements and talent pools change.

The thesis highlights the importance of ongoing evaluation and monitoring of AI tools to prevent unintended bias, but also notes that such monitoring is rare in practice.

4. Role Confusion for Recruiters and Hiring Managers

Finally, many AI initiatives are introduced without redefining what recruiters and hiring managers should do differently.

- Some recruiters fear replacement and disengage from AI tools, using them minimally or ignoring system suggestions.
- Others over-trust the tools, treating algorithmic scores as unquestionable and reducing their own critical evaluation.

The literature on technology acceptance underlines that perceived usefulness and ease of use, combined with organizational support, are central to adoption, but these are not always deliberately managed.

What Research Has Answered, and What It Still Misses

The academic and practitioner literature on AI in recruitment has grown rapidly. Multiple studies showcase how AI can automate repetitive tasks, reduce time-to-hire, and improve candidate-job matching. Yet several gaps remain, especially for Indian IT and ITeS organizations.

What We Already Know

- AI can significantly reduce manual screening time and support faster shortlisting, particularly in large organizations with high-volume hiring.
- Chatbots, social media analytics, and virtual reality experiences can improve engagement and innovation in specific contexts.
- HR leaders in larger firms often have a positive attitude toward AI, seeing it as a route to cost and process efficiency.

Where the Gaps Are

- **Regional and sector diversity.** Many studies are single-city or single-sector, limiting our understanding of how AI behaves across India's varied tech clusters and organizational sizes.
- **Long-term impact.** There is little longitudinal evidence on how AI-based recruitment affects retention, performance, or culture over time.
- **Ethical implementation.** Fairness, bias, privacy, and transparency are widely discussed conceptually, but there are few empirically tested frameworks showing how Indian firms actually implement ethical AI in recruitment.
- **Hybrid models.** While some authors call for a hybrid approach that combines technology with human judgment, there is limited concrete guidance on what this looks like in day-to-day practice.

This book is designed to sit precisely in that gap: it builds on the recognition that AI can be powerful, but focuses on **how** to use it responsibly and effectively in the Indian IT and ITeS context, grounded in broad-based empirical data.

A Practical Diagnostic: Is Your AI-Enabled Recruitment Under-Delivering?

Here is a simple diagnostic tool you can use with your leadership team. Each question is a yes/no or "to what extent" prompt.

1. **Process vs Tool**
    - Have you redesigned your hiring process end-to-end since introducing AI, or did you simply plug tools into existing steps?
2. **Candidate Communication**
    - Do candidates receive clear, timely information at every stage, including after AI-based assessments or rejections?
    - Do you explicitly explain where and how AI is used in your process?
3. **Fairness and Governance**
    - Do you regularly review AI-driven shortlisting and assessment outcomes for patterns of bias by gender, location, college tier, or experience level?

- Is there a documented process for candidates or employees to raise concerns about AI-based decisions?

4. **Recruiter Role and Readiness**
    - Have you clearly articulated how the recruiter's role changes with AI (what to stop, start, and continue)?
    - Have recruiters received hands-on training, not only on "how the tool works" but also on how to interpret and challenge AI outputs?
5. **Impact Measurement**
    - Beyond time-to-hire and cost-per-hire, are you tracking candidate experience and perceived fairness in AI-enabled processes regularly?

Check where you have gaps. Use this to drive your next leadership discussion.

AI Hiring Diagnostic: Is Your System Ready?

- [ ] **Process vs Tool**
  Have you redesigned your hiring process end-to-end since introducing AI?
- [x] **Candidate Communication**
  Do candidates receive clear, timely information at every stage?
- [x] **Fairness & Governance**
  Do you regularly review AI outcomes for bias patterns?
- [x] **Recruiter Role**
  Have you clearly articulated how recruiters' roles change with AI?
- [ ] **Impact Measurement**
  Are you tracking experience and fairness alongside efficiency?

If your answers reveal more gaps than strengths, your AI-enabled recruitment is likely under-delivering, not because the technology is incapable, but because the surrounding system is incomplete.

What This Means Before We Turn to the Data

Chapter 1 established why AI in talent acquisition has become a strategic imperative for India's IT and ITeS firms and why the stakes are high. Chapter 2 has explained why current approaches often fail to capture the full value of AI and sometimes create new risks.

In **Chapter 3**, we turn fully to the data. We will walk through the design of the study underpinning this book, who participated, what was measured, and how, and translate key statistical findings into practical insights that leaders and practitioners can act on immediately.

3

Inside the Evidence: What 556 Professionals and Candidates Revealed

The arguments in this book are not based on vendor promises or isolated case studies. They are grounded in a structured, empirical study of how AI-enabled recruitment tools are actually used and experienced in Indian IT and ITeS organizations.

This chapter opens that black box. It shows who participated in the study, what themes were examined, and what the findings mean in practical terms. If you are a CHRO, TA head, or HR tech builder, this chapter is the evidence base behind the playbooks that follow.

Who We Spoke To

The study drew on responses from 556 participants across India's IT and ITeS ecosystem: 286 recruitment professionals and 270 candidates. The professional group included recruiters, TA managers, HR business partners, and hiring managers. The candidate group included both early-career and experienced professionals who had recently gone through hiring processes for technology and operations roles. The sample was concentrated in India's six major IT and ITeS hubs, Bengaluru,

Hyderabad, Pune, Chennai, Delhi-NCR, and Mumbai, making the findings especially relevant for large and mid-sized firms operating in mainstream technology and outsourcing markets.

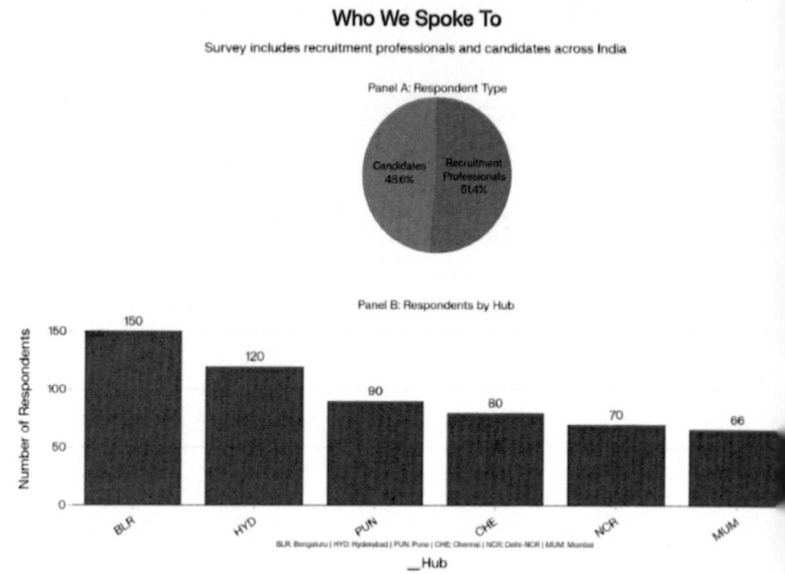

What We Examined

The study focused on a straightforward set of questions. Does AI-enabled recruitment help organizations hire faster and at lower cost? Does it improve recruiter efficiency? Does it improve candidate experience? And how do people perceive fairness when AI is part of the hiring process?

Key Constructs in the AI Hiring Research Model

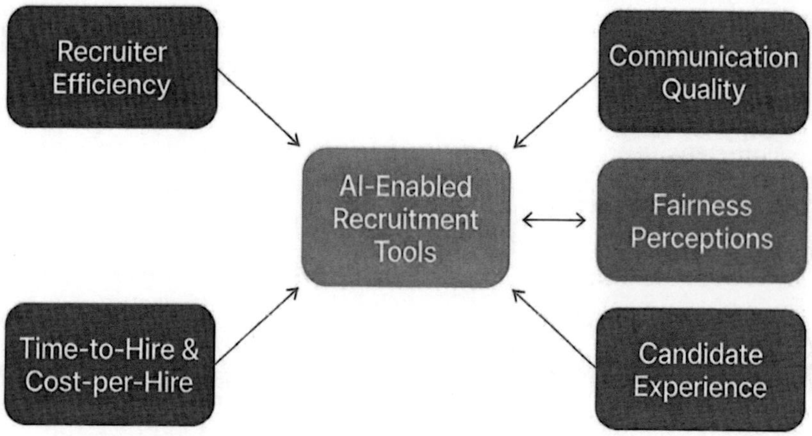

To answer these questions, the research looked at five broad areas: use of AI-enabled recruitment tools, recruiter efficiency, time-to-hire and cost-per-hire, candidate experience, and perceived fairness. Responses were gathered through structured survey items so that patterns could be compared across both professionals and candidates.

Research Snapshot

The study used a quantitative survey approach grounded in existing research on recruitment, technology adoption, and candidate experience. Separate but aligned questionnaires were used for professionals and candidates, and the survey instrument was tested before full rollout to improve clarity and consistency. In practical terms, that means the findings presented here are not based on anecdotes or vendor claims. They reflect recurring patterns across a large set of respondents with direct exposure to AI-enabled recruitment.

How to Read the Findings

At the simplest level, the study examined three connected ideas. First, whether AI-enabled recruitment improves recruiter efficiency and reduces time-to-hire and cost-per-hire. Second, whether candidate experience improves when technology is combined with strong communication. Third, whether people view these systems as fair, and under what conditions that trust becomes fragile.

The statistical testing behind these relationships is important, but for practitioners, the core message is clear and powerful: this study highlights the key areas where AI generates operational value, enhances user experience, and introduces governance risks if not properly managed. Understanding these dynamics is crucial for harnessing AI's potential while safeguarding against its pitfalls.

The Core Model in Simple Terms

The thesis proposed a research model connecting AI usage to key recruitment outcomes through several pathways. Simplified, it looks like this:

AI-enabled recruitment tools (e.g., screening, shortlisting, communication)

↓

Recruiter efficiency (how effectively recruiters can manage volume and tasks)

↓

Time-to-hire and cost-per-hire (how quickly and economically roles are filled)

In parallel:

AI-enabled recruitment tools

↓

Communication quality (frequency, clarity, and responsiveness of information to candidates)

↓

Candidate experience (trust, transparency, satisfaction)

Across these pathways, the study also examined perceived fairness, whether participants felt that AI-based processes were unbiased and just.

Simplified AI Hiring Impact Model

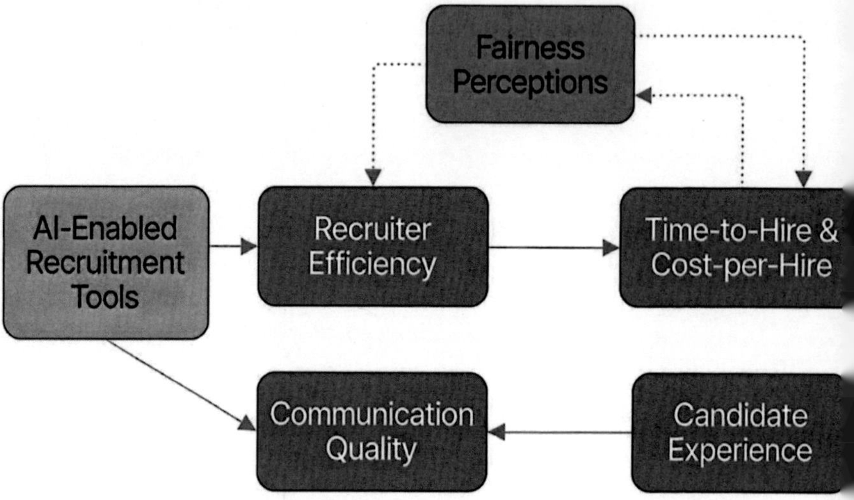

Multiple regression analyses were used to test these relationships (for example, whether higher AI use predicts higher efficiency, controlling for other factors), and mediation analysis was used to see whether communication quality acts as a bridge between technology and experience.

What We Found About Efficiency, Time, and Cost

The first set of findings speaks directly to the business case for AI.

AI and Recruiter Efficiency

Regression results showed that structured automation in resume screening and shortlisting had a strong, positive impact on recruiter efficiency, with a coefficient of 0.62, statistically significant at $p < 0.01$.

Figure 3.5 – Illustrative charts showing higher recruiter efficiency and reduced time and cost-to-hire associated with higher AI adoption, especially in ITeS

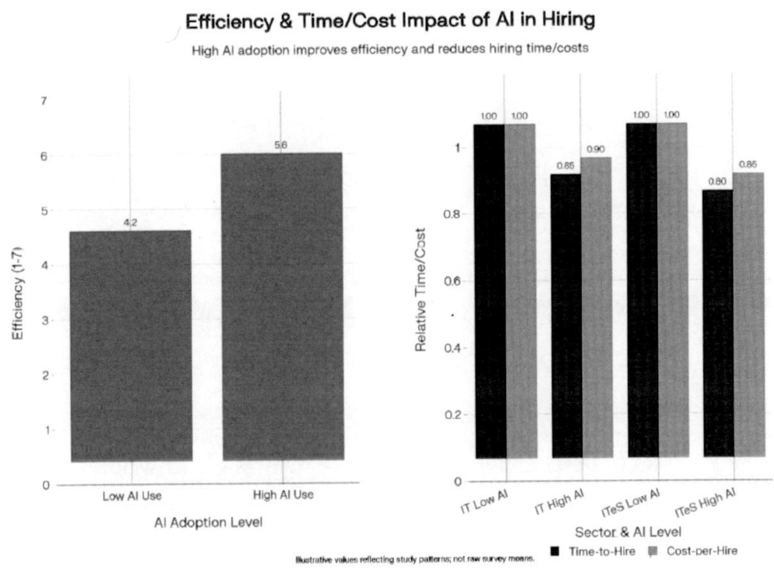

In plain language:

- As organizations increased their use of AI for initial screening and shortlisting, recruiters reported being able to process applications faster, manage more requisitions, and focus time on higher-value activities rather than repetitive filtering.

Professionals also reported increased productivity and perceived that AI tools improved efficiency across multiple stages of the recruitment cycle. As one recruiter reflected, "The system helps me get through volume faster, but I still need to decide what actually makes sense for the role." This balance between speed and judgment is a recurring theme in the data.

AI, Time-to-Hire, and Cost-per-Hire

Descriptive and inferential analysis highlighted that **AI use was significantly associated with reductions in time-to-hire and cost-per-hire**, particularly in ITeS organizations.

- ITeS firms, often dealing with large-scale, standardized hiring, experienced **stronger improvements** in these metrics than IT firms with more niche roles.
- Professionals widely agreed that AI tools reduced time to fill positions and helped bring down recruitment costs by automating routine steps and improving match quality.

From a leader's perspective, the takeaway is clear: when implemented in a structured way, AI in screening and shortlisting delivers measurable efficiency gains and cost savings, especially in high-volume environments.

What We Found About Candidate Experience

Efficiency gains alone are not enough if the process alienates the very people you want to hire. That is why the study paid particular attention to how candidates experienced AI-enabled recruitment.

The Central Role of Communication

The most important insight is that communication quality plays a decisive role in shaping candidate experience, with a mediation coefficient of 0.48.

This has two practical implications:

- **AI can improve candidate experience, but only when accompanied by clear, timely, and respectful communication.**
- **Without good communication, even advanced AI systems fail to generate positive experiences.** Candidates feel left in the dark.

How Communication Mediates AI's Impact on Candidate Experience

AI alone doesn't guarantee experience; communication quality is the key mediator

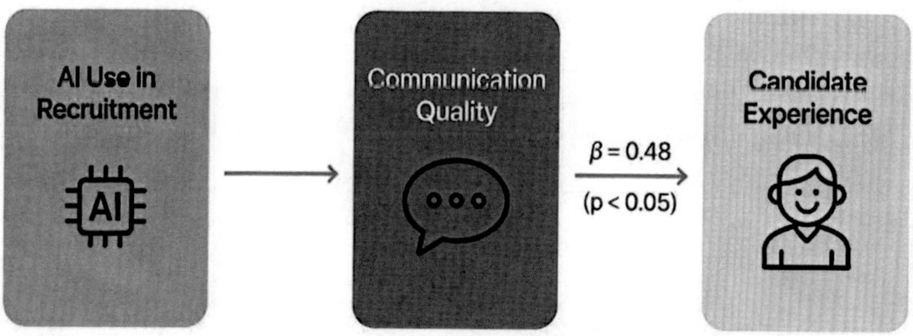

Candidates in the study reported higher trust, transparency, and satisfaction when:

- They knew what to expect at each stage of the process.
- They received prompt updates after key milestones (application, assessment, interview).

- They understood, at least broadly, how AI was being used to evaluate them.

Where these elements were missing, frustrations rose, even when the underlying process was faster than traditional hiring.

Professionals vs Candidates: Different Lenses

An interesting pattern in the data is how professionals and candidates prioritize different aspects:

- **Professionals** tend to emphasize efficiency, reduced time-to-hire, streamlined workflows, and lower costs as the main value of AI.
- **Candidates** value responsiveness and clarity, being kept informed, treated with respect, and given a sense of control over the process.

Both groups can report "satisfaction" with AI-enabled recruitment, but be talking about different experiences. Understanding this divergence is critical: it tells leaders that simply optimising for internal efficiency is not enough; candidate expectations must be designed into the system.

What We Found About Fairness and Bias

The study also explored how people perceive fairness in AI-enabled recruitment, an area where global debates are intense but local evidence has been limited.

General Perceptions of Fairness

Overall, both professionals and candidates tended to see AI tools as **largely fair and unbiased**.

- Many respondents agreed that AI helped standardize evaluation and reduce certain forms of subjective human bias.
- Candidates appreciated structured, criteria-based assessments when these were clearly communicated.

Across the study, most respondents rated fairness-related statements positively.

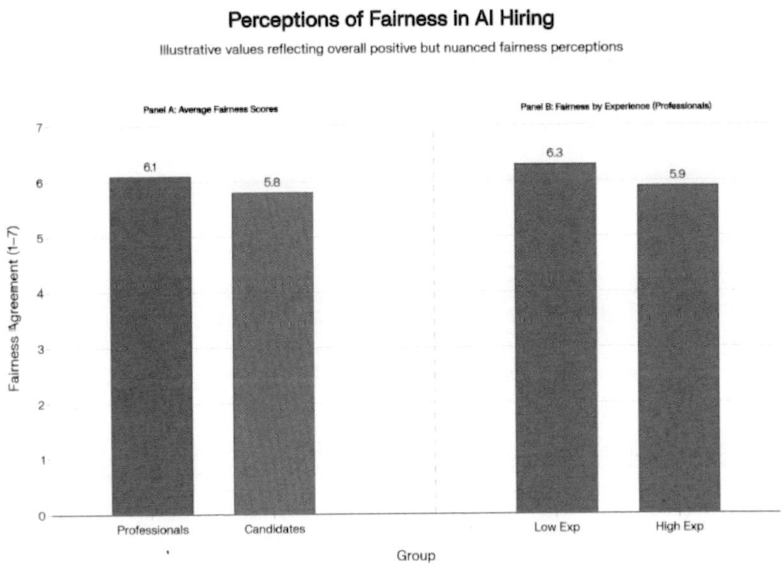

Awareness of Risks and Need for Monitoring

At the same time, the data reveals an undercurrent of caution:

- Some professionals agreed that AI tools could reinforce bias if not designed or monitored carefully, and supported regular evaluations of AI systems for fairness.

- Candidates indicated that being informed about AI use and knowing that systems were checked for bias contributed to their sense of trust.

Additional analysis across gender and experience bands shows differences in how fairness and bias risk are perceived, suggesting that one-size-fits-all communication about AI may not be sufficient.

For practitioners, it's important to understand that people are generally receptive to AI and often place more trust in it compared to human decision-making. However, this trust is delicate and relies heavily on transparency and effective governance.

Key Patterns at a Glance

Three patterns stand out from the study.

1. AI-enabled screening and shortlisting improve recruiter efficiency and help reduce time-to-hire and cost-per-hire, especially in high-volume ITeS environments.
2. Candidate experience improves only when automation is paired with clear and timely communication.
3. While most respondents view AI-enabled recruitment as broadly fair, formal monitoring and governance remain limited. One further tension is worth noting: professionals tend to value speed and efficiency most, while candidates care more about responsiveness and clarity.

These patterns shape the practical frameworks in the chapters that follow.

From Evidence to Action

Why include a full evidence chapter in a practitioner book? Because better decisions depend on better evidence.

This study offers three advantages over many existing narratives on AI in recruitment in India's IT and ITeS sectors:

1. It combines professional and candidate perspectives at meaningful scale.
2. It links AI use to concrete outcomes such as time, cost, efficiency, experience, and fairness.
3. It shows where AI works well on its own and where it depends on communication and governance to deliver value.

In the chapters that follow, we will translate this evidence into **design principles, process blueprints, and practical tools** you can use to reshape your own hiring systems.

- **Chapter 4** will show how to build an AI-first, human-centred hiring funnel that exploits the efficiency benefits highlighted here without sacrificing experience or fairness.
- **Chapter 5** will use the fairness insights to construct a simple but powerful framework for auditing and governing AI in recruitment.

The data tells us that AI in talent acquisition can deliver real value, but only when leaders move beyond buying tools and start designing systems. This chapter has shown you the evidence; the rest of the book will focus on the design.

4

Designing an AI-First, Human-Centred Hiring Funnel

As we reflect upon the above three chapters, a few things become absolutely clear.

1. When well-structured, AI can make recruitment faster and cheaper, especially when it is used for structured tasks like screening and shortlisting.
2. It is equally clear that AI alone does not guarantee a fair process and a better experience, those outcomes depend on how the entire hiring journey is designed, including communication, human intervention, and governance.

This chapter turns evidence into architecture. It explains how to create an **AI-first, human-centred hiring** process for IT and ITeS organizations that values what candidates and hiring managers care about: clarity, respect, and making good choices.

Principles for an AI-First, Human-Centred Funnel

Before touching tools or process maps, leaders need a set of design principles. Grounded in the findings from earlier chapters, four principles stand out.

Automate Volume, Not Relationships

Use AI to handle the work that scales badly for humans: triaging hundreds of resumes, matching profiles to role requirements, scheduling interviews across time zones, and sending status updates.

Do not use AI to eliminate the human moments that matter most: understanding nuanced fit, answering complex candidate questions, and building trust before critical decisions.

Design Around Communication

The study shows that communication quality mediates the relationship between technology use and candidate experience. That makes communication a **core system component**, not a cosmetic add-on.

Every step where AI makes or influences a decision must be accompanied by clear, timely, and respectful communication, or the experience benefits will not materialize.

Make Fairness a Feature, Not an Afterthought

Most participants perceived AI-based recruitment as fair, but very few organizations had structured fairness controls. Design the funnel so that fairness is actively monitored through data, checks, and process, rather than assumed.

Keep Humans in the Loop Where Judgment is Irreplaceable

AI performs best in structured, data-rich tasks with clear criteria. Human judgment is essential in ambiguous situations, in assessing cultural and contextual fit, and in final hiring decisions that affect teams and clients. The funnel should reflect this, with explicit human "checkpoints" baked in.

Case in Point: Scaling Hiring with Automation at Infosys

Infosys has invested heavily in automation to manage high-volume hiring, especially for early-career and lateral roles. By combining online assessments, automated screening, and structured workflows, the organisation reduced manual screening effort and improved consistency in shortlisting.

The key lesson is not the tools themselves, but how they are integrated. Automation works best when it is embedded into a clearly defined funnel, with human review focused on edge cases and final decisions. This aligns with the broader principle in this chapter: AI delivers value when it is part of a designed system, not an add-on.

Mapping the Modern Funnel: Stage by Stage

An AI-first, human-centred funnel for IT and ITeS typically has six major stages:

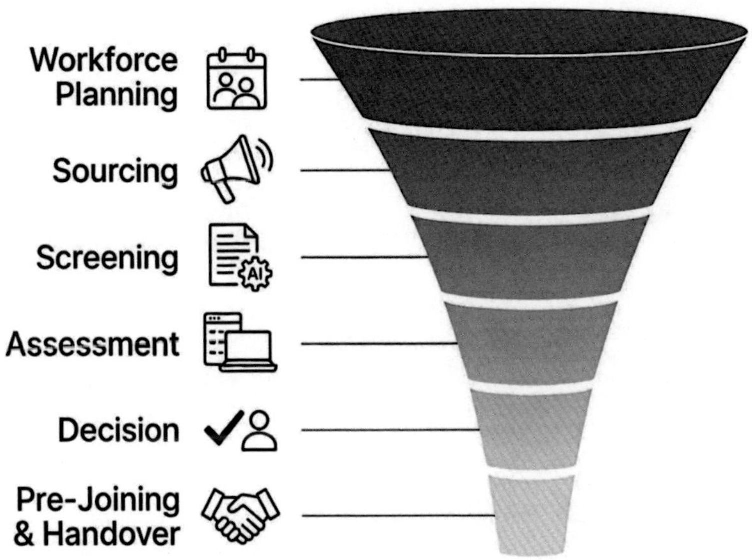

Below, we look at each stage, explaining **where AI fits, where humans add most value**, and **what to watch out for**.

Stage 1 – Workforce Planning and Requisition

What usually happens:
Business leaders share headcount plans. HR translates these into job descriptions and requisitions. TA uses historical data and intuition to estimate timelines.

How AI can help:

- Predictive analytics can forecast demand based on historical hiring patterns, attrition trends, and pipeline data.
- Skills analytics can reveal emerging gaps (for example, demand moving from generic Java roles to specific cloud-native skill sets).

Human-centred elements:

- HR and TA leaders validate predictions against strategic priorities and client pipelines.
- Hiring managers refine role definitions to ensure they are realistic and not copy-pasted from legacy templates.

Design watchpoints:

- Do not let models set unrealistic expectations ("the system says 10 days to fill") without human review.
- Ensure requisitions are written in a way AI tools can interpret (clear must-have vs nice-to-have skills) without excluding diverse profiles unnecessarily.

Stage 2 – Sourcing and Attraction

What usually happens:
Jobs are posted on portals, LinkedIn, and internal career sites; recruiters may mine databases manually.

How AI can help:

- AI-enabled sourcing engines can search internal and external databases to identify candidates matching defined criteria.
- Programmatic advertising can optimize job ad placements based on past performance, time of day, and channel effectiveness.

Human-centred elements:

- Recruiters craft narratives that explain the role, culture, and growth opportunities beyond generic text.
- TA and marketing teams collaborate on employer branding content that speaks to the real concerns of tech professionals.

Design watchpoints:

- Guard against over-reliance on narrow keyword matches that exclude non-traditional career paths.
- Periodically review which channels and criteria your AI sourcing favours to avoid homogeneity in talent pools.

Stage 3 – Screening and Shortlisting

This is where the study found AI had the strongest measurable impact on efficiency. Structured automation in resume screening and shortlisting improved operational efficiency with a coefficient of 0.62 ($p < 0.01$).

What usually happens:

AI parses resume, scores candidates against job requirements, and flags a shortlist. Recruiters review this shortlist and decide whom to move forward.

How AI can help:

- **Resume parsing and matching:** Extracting skills, experience, and qualifications, then scoring candidates against standardized role profiles.
- **Rule-based filters:** Applying basic eligibility rules automatically (location, notice period, salary bands, required certifications).
- **Duplicate checking:** Identifying candidates who already exist in the system to avoid confusion and over-contact.

Human-centred elements:

- Recruiters review AI shortlists, spot-check rejections, and override the system where context justifies it.
- They pay special attention to candidates with non-linear career paths or unconventional backgrounds.

Design watchpoints:

- Ensure that the criteria used for scoring are well-defined and defensible; avoid proxies that encode bias (e.g., college tier as a primary predictor of success).
- Periodically sample "rejected" candidates to see if strong profiles are being filtered out incorrectly.

- Communicate clearly to candidates that AI is used for initial matching, and that recruiters review shortlisted profiles.

Stage 3: AI Screening & Shortlisting Blueprint

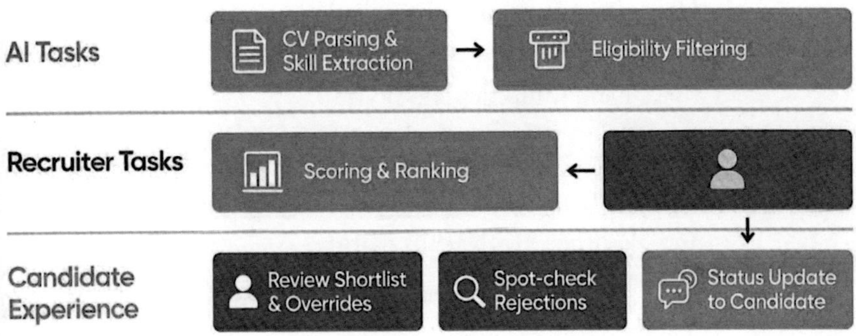

Stage 4 – Assessment and Interviews

What usually happens:
Candidates may complete online technical tests, coding challenges, or situational judgment tests. Some organizations use asynchronous video interviews for the early stages. Interviewers then conduct live technical and behavioural rounds.

How AI can help:

- **Adaptive assessments:** Tests that adjust difficulty based on responses, providing a more precise view of skill level.
- **Structured video interviews:** Platforms that present standardized questions, capture responses, and sometimes offer basic analytics to assist reviewers.

- **Scheduling automation:** Systems that match interviewer and candidate availability across time zones and send reminders.

Human-centred elements:

- Hiring managers and interview panels interpret assessment results, probe deeper in live discussions, and triangulate multiple data points.
- Interviewers evaluate contextual fit: problem-solving approach, collaboration style, client-handling potential, and alignment with team culture.

Design watchpoints:

- Avoid using opaque "black-box" scoring in high-stakes decisions without human review.
- Provide candidates with clear information about how assessments will be used and what success looks like.
- Train interviewers to use assessment outputs as inputs, not as verdicts, to avoid over-reliance on scores.

Stage 5 – Decision and Offer

What usually happens:
Panels submit feedback. TA consolidates inputs. Hiring managers make final decisions, and offers are extended.

How AI can help:

- **Decision support dashboards:** Aggregating assessment scores, interviewer ratings, and historical data to highlight patterns and potential risks.
- **Offer modelling:** Suggesting compensation ranges based on internal equity and market trends.

Human-centred elements:

- Final hiring decisions remain with human leaders, who consider business context and potential beyond the data on file.
- TA partners and hiring managers discuss edge cases where indicators are mixed.

Design watchpoints:

- Ensure decisions are documented with clear rationales that go beyond "the system showed a high fit score."
- Watch for subtle bias, such as consistently discounting candidates from certain backgrounds despite strong assessment results, and address it through structured decision criteria

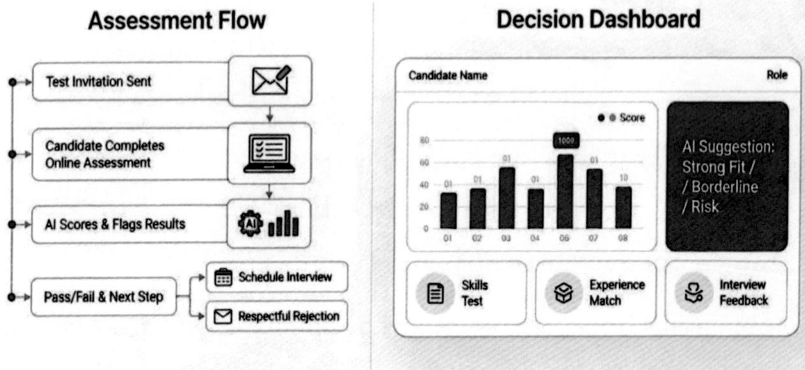

Stage 6 – Pre-Joining and Onboarding Handoff

What usually happens:

After the offer, candidates receive joining formalities, background checks, and limited engagement until their first day. Drop-outs at this stage are common.

How AI can help:

- **Nudging and engagement:** Automated reminders, FAQs, and personalized content to keep candidates engaged through notice periods.
- **Risk alerts:** Predictive signals flagging candidates at high risk of backing out based on activity patterns.

Human-centred elements:

- TA or hiring managers schedule personal check-ins for critical hires.
- Teams begin integration early, with introductions to future peers, mentors, or project leads.

Design watchpoints:

- Avoid turning the post-offer stage into a flood of automated messages; maintain a balance of digital and personal touches.
- Be transparent about what data you track and why, especially in predictive models that flag "risk of drop-out."

Two Blueprint Examples: ITeS and IT

Because the research found stronger time and cost benefits in ITeS than in IT, it is useful to look at two simplified blueprints that reflect these differences.

Blueprint A – High-Volume ITeS Roles

Context:
Customer support, transaction processing, and voice/non-voice operations, where large numbers of similar roles must be filled quickly.

AI emphasis: High, especially in sourcing, screening, assessment, and communication.

Key design features:

- Automated sourcing from talent pools and job portals.
- AI-based eligibility filtering and matching at scale.
- Standardized online assessments for language, aptitude, or process skills.
- Automated communication for most candidates, with human interaction reserved for final stages and exceptions.

Human-centred safeguards:

- Regular fairness audits of screening and assessment outcomes by gender, location, and educational background.
- Human review of a sample of auto-rejected profiles.
- Clear explanation to candidates about the process, timeline, and assessment criteria.

Blueprint B – Niche IT Specialist Roles

Context:
Cloud architects, data scientists, senior developers, product managers, and other roles where talent pools are smaller and fit is nuanced.

AI emphasis: Moderate; focused more on sourcing, information consolidation, and coordination than on automated decision-making.

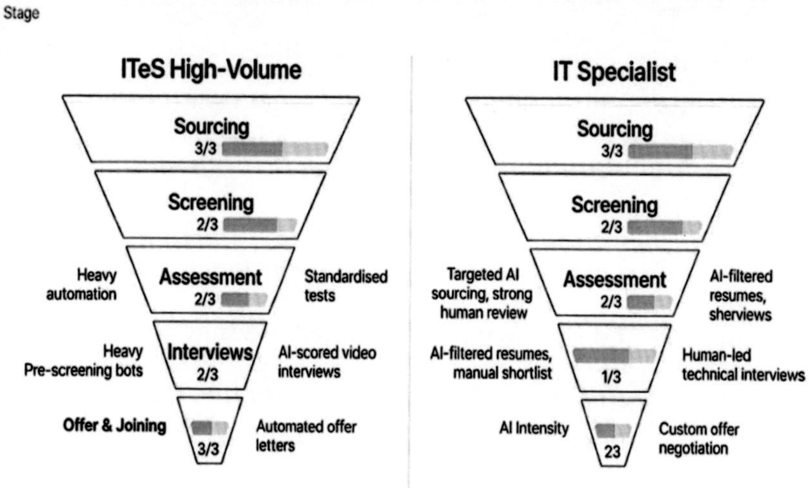

Key design features:

- AI-enabled sourcing to identify candidates with rare skill combinations across networks and databases.
- Resume parsing to structure information for easier comparison, but not to auto-eliminate.
- Use of AI for scheduling and note consolidation from interviews.

Human-centred safeguards:

- Recruiters and hiring managers manually review almost all applications flagged by AI sourcing.
- Emphasis on live technical and behavioural interviews for final decisions.
- Deliberate investment in personal communication, especially for passive candidates.

Building Communication into the Funnel

Given the mediation effect identified in the research, communication needs to be designed as rigorously as any algorithm.

For each stage, ask:

1. **What decision or action happens here?**
2. **What does the candidate need to know, and when?**
3. **Which parts of that communication can be automated, and which should come from a human?**

Communication Built into Every Stage

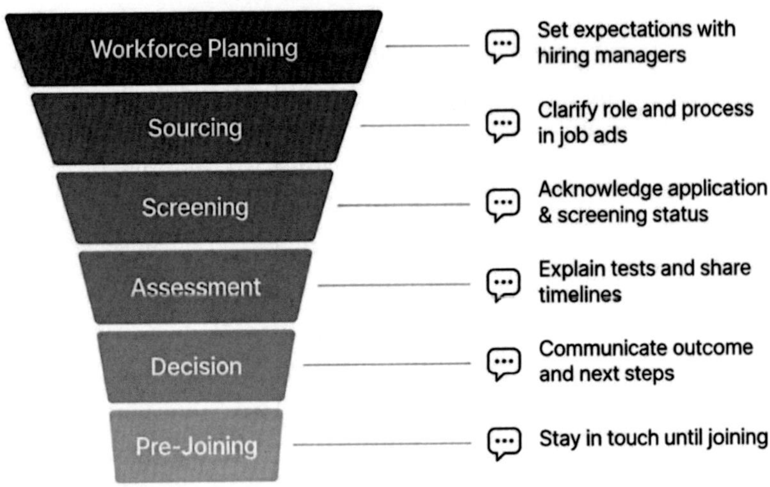

Examples of good practice:

- **Application acknowledgement:** Immediate, automated, but personalized enough to feel human, explaining next steps and typical timelines.

- **Post-screening updates:** Clear notification if the candidate is moving forward, including what tools (AI or otherwise) were used and what they should expect next.
- **Post-assessment feedback:** Even if detailed feedback is not possible at scale, provide basic information, whether they met cut-offs, and how long it will take to hear about next steps.
- **Closure:** Respectful, timely rejection messages that thank candidates for their time and invite them to stay in a talent community where appropriate.

The difference between a "cold" AI process and a human-centred one often comes down to how well these messages are designed and delivered.

Guardrails: Where Humans Must Stay in Control

Finally, no matter how advanced your AI stack becomes, there are lines you should not cross.

- **Final hiring decisions** should always rest with accountable human leaders.
- **Sensitive judgments**, such as assessing potential for leadership, client engagement, or cross-cultural work, should be heavily human-led, with AI as input at best.
- **Exception handling** (for candidates with unusual profiles, career breaks, or non-standard pathways) requires human discretion.

The study's findings, that professionals value efficiency while candidates value responsiveness and clarity, remind us that recruitment is not just a data-processing exercise; it is a relationship-building function.

From Architecture to Implementation

Designing an AI-first, human-centred funnel is a strategic exercise, but it should lead quickly to practical changes. Use this chapter as a checklist:

- Have you mapped your current funnel and explicitly marked where AI is used, where humans decide, and where communication happens?
- Are you using AI in the stages where the research suggests it has the highest efficiency impact (screening and shortlisting), with appropriate human oversight?
- Have you treated communication as a core design layer, given its proven role in shaping candidate experience?
- Do your blueprints differ for high-volume ITeS roles and niche IT roles, reflecting the different benefits and risks identified in the data?

In **Chapter 5**, we build on this architecture to focus on one critical dimension: fairness. You will learn how to put in place simple but robust fairness audits, transparency practices, and governance mechanisms so that your AI-enabled funnel is not only efficient and engaging, but also trustworthy and compliant.

5

Building Fair and Transparent AI in Recruitment

AI can help Indian IT and ITeS organizations hire faster and more efficiently, but without deliberate safeguards, it can just as easily hard-code old prejudices into new systems. The research behind this book shows that while most professionals and candidates *perceive* AI-based recruitment as fair, very few organizations have robust processes to test, monitor, or explain that fairness.

This chapter turns fairness from a vague aspiration into an operational practice. It explains what fairness means in recruitment, where bias sneaks into AI-driven systems, and how to set up a simple fairness and transparency framework that your TA team can run without a PhD in data science.

What Fairness Really Means in AI-Enabled Recruitment

In the study, respondents generally agreed that AI tools evaluate candidates objectively and treat people consistently. However, when probed about monitoring, many also agreed that AI systems should be regularly assessed for bias, and that candidates ought to be informed about how these tools are used. This reveals a key nuance: people **want to trust** AI, but they also **expect** it to be governed.

For practical purposes, fairness in AI-enabled recruitment has three dimensions:

1. **Procedural fairness** – Are processes consistent, transparent, and respectful?
2. **Distributive fairness** – Are opportunities and outcomes (shortlists, offers) reasonably balanced across relevant groups?
3. **Informational fairness** – Do candidates receive honest, timely explanations about what is happening and why?

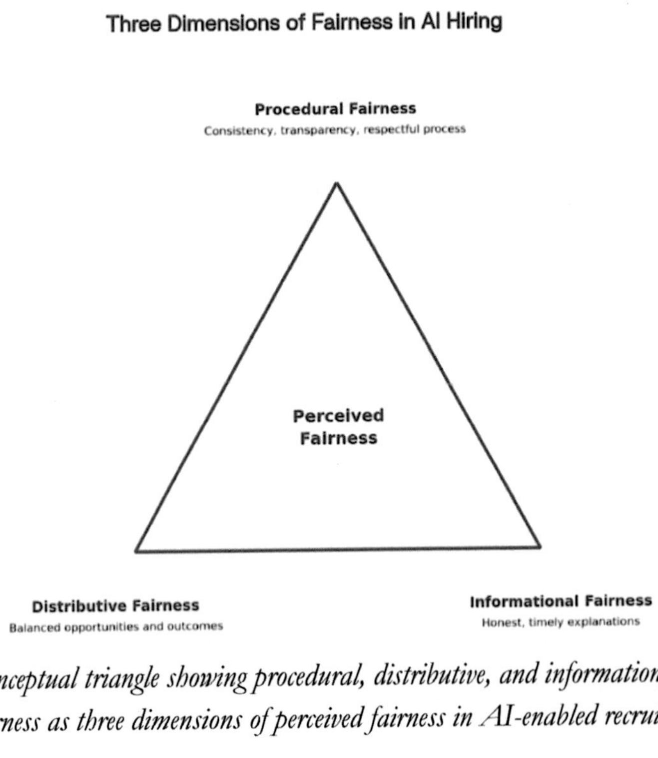

Conceptual triangle showing procedural, distributive, and informational fairness as three dimensions of perceived fairness in AI-enabled recruitment.

As we have discussed in the previous chapters, the research strongly clarifies that candidate experience improves through effective communication even in AI-heavy processes. Conversely, even technically sound models can feel unfair if the process is opaque.

Where Bias Creeps Into AI-Enabled Hiring

Globally, studies and case reports have warned that AI trained on historical hiring data can reproduce or amplify existing bias. In India's diverse labour market, the risk is heightened by stratification along gender, education, region, language, and socio-economic lines.

The landscape of regulatory oversight is evolving significantly. Lawmakers and regulators are increasingly recognizing that the use of AI in hiring processes extends beyond mere technical considerations; it now encompasses critical issues of rights, accountability, and governance. For employers, this shift means that the fundamental question has transformed: it's no longer about whether an AI tool enhances speed or efficiency. Instead, it's about whether that tool can be transparently explained, effectively monitored, rigorously challenged, and robustly defended when its outcomes impact individuals' opportunities for employment.

Bias can slip in at several points:

- **Training data:** If historical hiring skewed toward certain colleges, cities, or demographics, algorithms trained on that data may prefer similar profiles, even without explicitly using those attributes.

- **Feature selection:** Using certain proxies, such as college tier, years of continuous experience, or language cues, as indicators of quality can inadvertently disadvantage specific groups.
- **Model deployment:** Even a well-designed model can become biased if it is used for different roles or regions than those it was trained for, or if the underlying talent market changes.
- **Human interaction with AI:** Recruiters may over-trust AI scores and under-challenge suggestions, or conversely use AI selectively in ways that reinforce their own biases.

Case in Point: When AI Reinforces Bias

One of the most widely cited examples is Amazon's experimental hiring algorithm, which was found to disadvantage certain profiles because it was trained on historical hiring data that reflected past biases. The system was eventually discontinued.

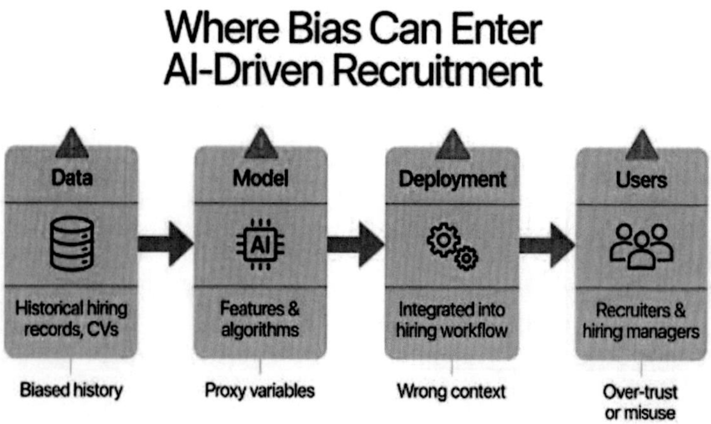

The lesson is clear: AI does not remove bias by default. Without active monitoring and correction, it can replicate and even amplify existing patterns. This is why fairness audits and governance mechanisms are essential, not optional.

A Simple Fairness Audit Framework

To move from concern to action, organizations need a fairness audit that is **simple, repeatable, and understandable** for TA and HR teams. Based on the study's findings and the broader literature, you can implement a five-step loop.

Step 1 – Define Relevant Groups and Outcomes

Start by deciding **which groups and outcomes you will monitor**. For Indian IT and ITeS, typical group dimensions include:

- Gender
- Location (metro vs non-metro, specific regions)
- College category (top-tier vs other institutions)
- Experience band (fresher, mid-level, senior)

Key outcomes to track:

- Application-to-shortlist rates
- Shortlist-to-interview rates
- Interview-to-offer rates
- Offer acceptance and joining rates

The study's demographic breakdowns (gender, years of experience, company size, location) already provide a template for such segmentation.

Step 2 – Compare Outcomes Across Groups

On a regular cadence (e.g., quarterly), pull data and compare these outcomes between groups for roles where AI has a significant influence (especially in screening and shortlisting).

You are not looking for perfect equality, but for **unexplained gaps**. For example:

- Do women with similar qualifications get shortlisted at meaningfully lower rates than men?
- Do candidates from non-metro locations consistently appear less in shortlists than expected, given the application pool?

The thesis demonstrates how ANOVA and regression techniques can reveal differences across gender and experience; you can apply the same logic at a more basic, dashboard-driven level.

Step 3 – Investigate Potential Causes

If you find concerning discrepancies, investigate both the **data** and the **process**:

- Are certain keywords or criteria (e.g., continuous employment, specific institutions) indirectly causing bias?

- Is AI being used differently for certain regions or channels (for example, only auto-screening campus applicants from selected colleges)?
- Are recruiters overriding AI more often in favour of particular profiles?

The goal is not to "blame the algorithm," but to understand **how configuration and usage** might create unfair patterns.

Step 4 – Adjust Rules, Models, or Processes

Based on what you learn, you may need to:

- Adjust AI scoring criteria (down-weighting or removing biased proxies).
- Add constraints (for example, ensuring a minimum representation of diverse profiles at the shortlisting stage, provided they meet baseline criteria).
- Refine job descriptions or sourcing strategies that inadvertently limit diversity.

The empirical foundation of your study, showing that AI can improve efficiency without reducing perceptions of fairness, supports the case that fairness adjustments can be made without abandoning automation.

Step 5 – Document and Communicate

Finally, document:

- What you checked
- What you found
- What you changed

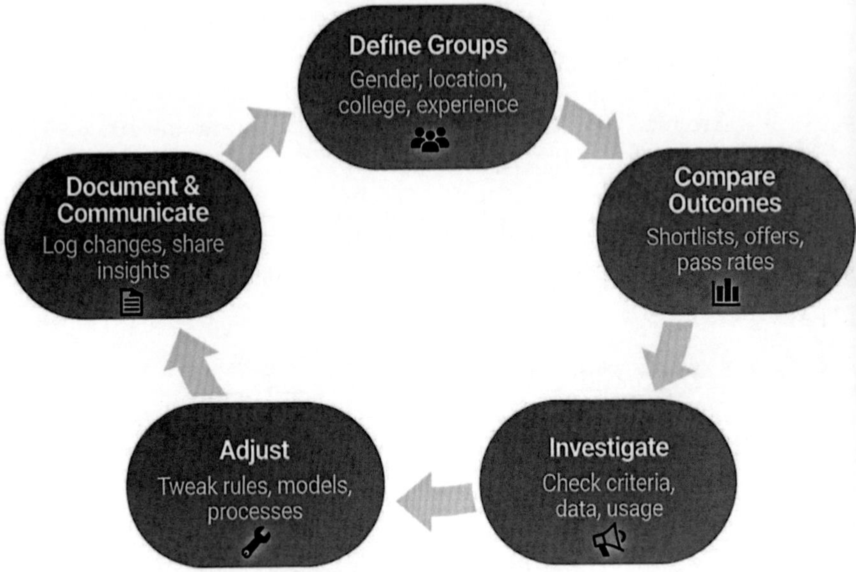

Repeat each quarter for critical roles

Internally, this builds trust with TA, HR, and leadership. Externally, it allows you to talk credibly about responsible AI-enabled recruitment when candidates or clients ask. The study's finding that candidates value transparency and monitoring of AI for fairness directly reinforces this step.

Making Transparency Part of the Candidate Experience

The research findings, as discussed in the earlier chapters, show that transparent and prompt communication leads to a better experience for candidates. Fairness is not just about balanced numbers; it is about **how** the process is explained.

What Candidates Want to Know

Based on candidate responses in the study and broader practice, candidates typically want clarity on:

- **Where AI is used.** Is it in resume screening, assessments, scheduling, or all of the above?
- **How decisions are made.** Is AI making final decisions, or is it assisting human recruiters?
- **What they can do to prepare.** Are there specific competencies being assessed, and how will they be evaluated?
- **How their data is treated.** Who has access to it, how long it is stored, and whether it is used beyond the current recruitment process.

Organisations that pre-emptively answer these questions, through FAQs, process overviews, and honest responses during interactions, build a sense of informational fairness that improves candidate experience, even when outcomes are not favourable.

How We Use AI in Hiring

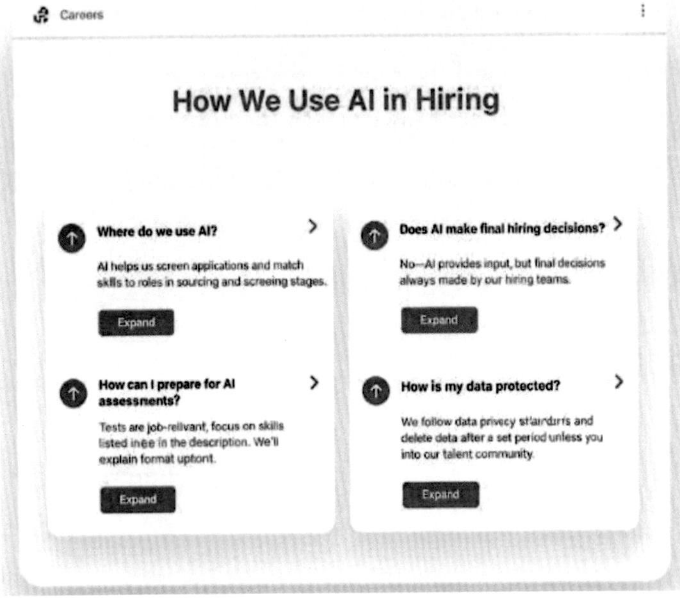

Sample Communication Elements

You can incorporate transparency through:

- A short section on your careers site titled "How We Use AI in Hiring," written in plain language.
- Automated messages that state, for example: "Your resume has been screened using a combination of AI tools and human review to check alignment with the skills and experience required for this role."
- Interview invitations that explain how earlier assessment scores will be used by interviewers.

- Rejection emails that, where possible, indicate if candidates did not meet specific thresholds rather than giving generic statements.

These steps directly address the gap highlighted in the research: AI processes that are high-tech but low-communication are experienced as impersonal and opaque, damaging trust even when they are efficient.

Governance: Policies, Roles, and Escalation Paths

Fairness and transparency cannot rest on individual goodwill; they require **governance**.

Policy Foundations

At a minimum, organizations should define:

- **An AI in Recruitment Policy** that outlines:
    - Where AI may be used, and for what purposes.
    - Principles of fairness, non-discrimination, and respect for candidates.
    - Requirements for periodic audits and documentation.
- **Data and Privacy Guidelines** clarifying:
    - What candidate data is collected and processed by AI tools.

- How consent is obtained and how data retention is managed.

Governance RACI for AI in Recruitment

Roles and responsibilities matrix for AI implementation

Activity	TA Leadership	HR Analytics	IT / Vendor	Recruiters & Hiring Managers
Tool Selection	R/A	C	C	I
Configuration	A	C	R	I
Monitoring & Fairness Audits	A	R	C	C
Candidate Communication	A	C	I	R
Issue Escalation	A	C	C	R

R = Responsible (does the work)
A = Accountable (owns the outcome)
C = Consulted (provides input)
I = Informed (kept updated)

These align with concerns raised in the literature around algorithmic bias, privacy, and accountability in technology-enabled recruitment. Recent legal actions make these risks tangible. In the United States, the EEOC's case against iTutorGroup alleged that the company programmed its hiring software to automatically reject older applicants, and the matter was later settled. In a separate and closely watched case, U.S. courts allowed key discrimination claims to proceed against Workday over allegations that AI-enabled screening tools disadvantaged applicants on grounds including age, race, and disability. These cases do not prove that every hiring algorithm is biased, but they do show that employers and technology providers can face real legal scrutiny when automated systems influence access to jobs.

Clear Roles and Responsibilities

Governance also requires assigning responsibility:

- **TA leadership** – accountable for process design, tool selection, and ensuring fairness audits happen.
- **HR analytics/data teams** – responsible for running analyses and reporting patterns.
- **Vendors and IT** – responsible for technical documentation, change logs, and support.
- **Recruiters and hiring managers** – responsible for using AI outputs appropriately and escalating concerns when something seems off.

The research indicates that without clear ownership, organizations tend to under-monitor AI even when they conceptually recognize the risk of bias.

Escalation and Appeals

Finally, there should be straightforward ways for:

- **Candidates** to ask questions or raise concerns about AI-based decisions.
- **Employees** to report suspected unfairness in how tools are configured or used.

Even if these are used rarely, their existence reinforces trust and signals seriousness about fairness.

Fairness Without Paralysis: Striking the Balance

A common fear among practitioners is that focusing on fairness will slow down hiring or make AI projects unmanageable. The evidence from the study suggests the opposite: AI can deliver efficiency gains **and** preserve perceptions of fairness when implementation is thoughtful.

Several points from the research support a balanced view:

- Professionals and candidates already view AI in recruitment positively, especially when it reduces repetitive tasks and introduces structure.
- Candidate experience, including perceptions of fairness, improves when communication is strong, a change that often costs time and attention, not heavy technology.
- There is room to introduce monitoring and governance now, before serious failures or public controversies arise, which is far less disruptive than reacting after the fact. The wider regulatory and litigation landscape only strengthens that case. Waiting until scrutiny arrives is usually more expensive than building responsible controls early.

The goal is not to create perfect equality in all outcomes. No hiring system can do that. The goal is to **show that your process is intentional, monitored, and responsive**.

From Fairness Principles to Daily Practice

To close this chapter, consider a quick self-check for your organisation:

- Do you know **where** AI currently influences candidate outcomes in your funnel?
- Have you ever run a **basic fairness check** on those stages, comparing shortlisting or assessment outcomes across gender, location, or other relevant groups?
- Is there a **clear explanation** of AI usage visible to candidates and employees?
- Do your recruiters know **how to handle candidate questions** about AI and fairness?
- Are there **documented responsibilities** and a simple escalation path if someone suspects unfair patterns?

If the answer to several of these questions is "no," your AI-enabled recruitment practices likely rely more on hopeful trust than on demonstrable fairness. The good news is that the steps described in this chapter are achievable without massive technical investment; they primarily require clarity, discipline, and leadership will.

In **Chapter 6**, we turn to the people most directly affected by these changes inside the organization: recruiters. You will see how AI reshapes their role, what new skills they need, and how to transform them into data-savvy, fairness-conscious talent partners who can bring the principles of this chapter to life in everyday hiring.

6

Turning Recruiters into AI-Powered Talent Partners

Technology is changing recruitment, but its biggest impact is not replacement. It is a role transformation. As outlined in Chapter 4, AI-enabled hiring systems shift much of the transactional workload away from recruiters. What remains, and what grows in importance, is judgment, communication, and decision-making. This chapter focuses on that shift: how recruiters evolve into AI-powered talent partners, what new skills they need, and how organisations can build those capabilities deliberately.

The New Role of the Recruiter

Historically, recruiters in IT and ITeS organisations spent much of their time on manual work: scanning resumes, chasing schedules, updating spreadsheets, and sending routine emails. The research shows that AI-enabled talent partners now take over a large portion of this repetitive workload, especially in resume screening, shortlisting, and basic communication.

This shift opens the door to a different profile of recruiter: **the AI-powered talent partner** who:

- Interprets data from AI systems instead of generating it manually.
- Advises hiring managers on market realities and process design.
- Curates candidate experience across automated and human touchpoints.
- Helps protect fairness and transparency in how AI is used.

Yesterday	Today
Manual CV screening	Interpreting AI shortlists
Chasing schedules by email	Consulting hiring managers
Updating spreadsheets	Using dashboards & data
Reactive candidate communication	Owning candidate experience

In other words, the recruiter's value moves **up** the stack, from transactional processing to strategic judgment and relationship-building.

What the Data Says About Recruiter Experience with AI

The professional side of the survey offers important clues about how recruiters are already experiencing AI.

- A large majority of professionals agreed that AI tools reduce time to fill roles and improve shortlisting quality, reflecting the strong statistical link between automation and efficiency (coefficient 0.62, $p < 0.01$)
- Respondents also associated AI with **higher productivity** and **better transparency** when tools were integrated effectively into their workflows.
- At the same time, the literature and qualitative feedback highlight concerns about **complexity, lack of training**, and **uncertainty about how decisions are made**, especially when AI systems are introduced without clear guidance.

These mixed signals tell us two things:

1. Recruiters are largely **open to AI** when it demonstrably helps them.
2. Their potential is constrained when AI is imposed without clarity, training, or a redefinition of their role.

The rest of this chapter shows how to address these constraints.

Core Competencies of an AI-Powered Recruiter

To thrive in an AI-enabled TA function, recruiters need a blend of **technical fluency, data literacy, and human skills**. The research and broader literature suggest several critical competencies.

Tool Fluency and Process Understanding

Recruiters need to be comfortable with:

- How AI-enabled ATS, screening tools, and assessment platforms operate in the hiring funnel.
- What each tool is good at (e.g., parsing, scoring, matching) and where its limitations lie.
- How data flows across systems, from application to offer, and where errors or delays can occur.

This is not about learning to code; it is about understanding **capabilities and constraints** so they can use tools intelligently.

Data Literacy

Because AI outputs are data-driven, recruiters must be able to:

- Read and interpret **basic analytics** (conversion rates, channel effectiveness, time-to-stage metrics).
- Spot anomalies, for example, unusual drops at a particular stage or for a particular candidate segment.
- Ask informed questions when something "doesn't look right."

Your study's emphasis on measurable outcomes, time-to-hire, cost-per-hire, efficiency, experience, and fairness provides a natural set of metrics that recruiters can learn to monitor.

Communication and Candidate Advocacy

Candidates in the research valued responsiveness, clarity, and transparency above almost everything else in AI-enabled processes. That makes **communication** a central recruiter skill:

- Explaining the overall process and where AI is used.
- Setting expectations about timelines and next steps.
- Delivering difficult messages, such as rejections, with respect and context.

Recruiters also become **advocates** for candidates' perspectives when designing or tweaking AI-driven processes, ensuring systems do not ignore the human experience.

Fairness Awareness and Ethical Judgment

As Chapter 5 outlined, fairness in AI is not automatic. Recruiters have a critical role to play in:

- Noticing patterns that may indicate bias (e.g., similar profiles being rejected repeatedly at AI stages).
- Escalating concerns about parameters or outputs that feel misaligned.
- Participating in audits by providing context and examples from real cases.

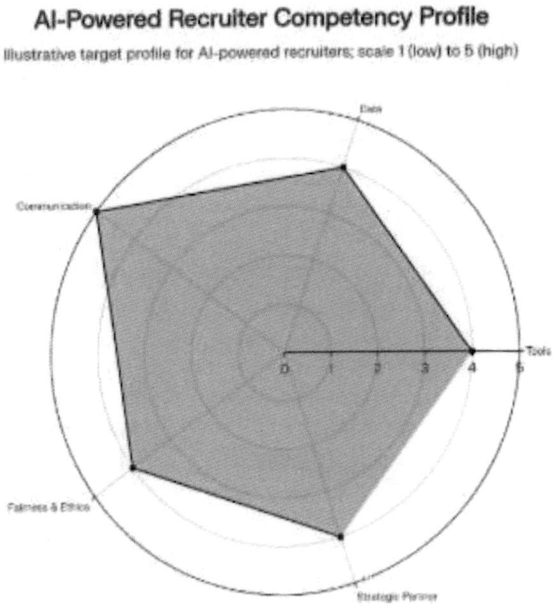

They do not need to run statistical tests, but they must be alert to fairness issues and know what to do when they see them.

AI Literacy: The Non-Negotiable Capability

As AI becomes embedded in hiring, a new baseline capability is emerging: AI literacy. This does not mean technical expertise or model-building. It means understanding how AI systems make recommendations, what data they rely on, and where they can go wrong.

In practical terms, AI-literate recruiters can:

1. Understand how matching, ranking, and scoring systems work at a conceptual level.
2. Recognise the difference between signal and proxy (for example, skills vs institutional pedigree).
3. Identify when outputs seem inconsistent with role requirements or candidate context.
4. Explain AI-assisted decisions to candidates and hiring managers in simple, credible terms.

Without this literacy, recruiters either over-trust the system or disengage from it. With it, they become informed users who can challenge, refine, and improve AI-enabled processes.

From Transactional to Advisory: Redesigning the Recruiter's Day

Shifting to an AI-powered recruiter model is not only about training. It is about redefining how recruiters spend their time once automation takes over repetitive tasks.

A "Before and After" View

Yesterday	Today
Manual CV screening	Interpreting AI shortlists
Chasing schedules by email	Consulting hiring managers
Updating spreadsheets	Using dashboards & data
Reactive candidate communication	Owning candidate experience

Before AI:

- Large blocks of time spent screening resumes manually.
- Constant coordination via email and calls to fix interview slots.
- Ad hoc, reactive communication with candidates; many inquiries about status.
- Limited ability to analyse where the process is breaking down.

After AI (when well implemented):

- AI handles initial screening, freeing time to review edge cases and calibrate profiles.
- Scheduling assistants and workflow tools manage most coordination.
- Recruiters proactively communicate with candidates at key points in the journey.
- Dashboards show where candidates drop off, which channels work best, and how long each stage takes.

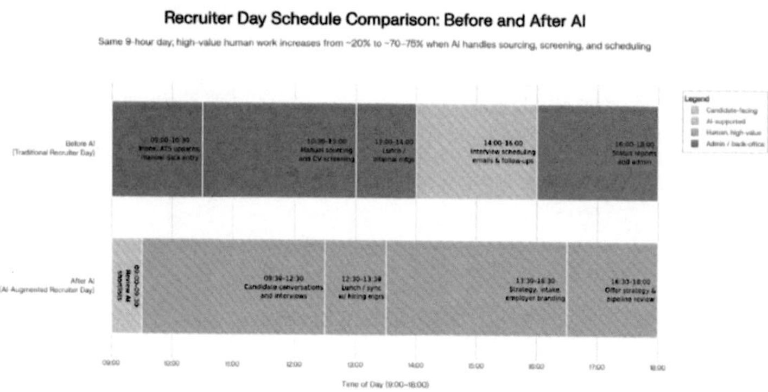

In the second scenario, recruiters' calendars shift from being dominated by repetitive tasks to a mix of **consultation, analysis, and relationship-building**.

One recruiter described the shift this way: "Earlier, my day was all about screening and coordination. Now I spend more time with hiring managers and candidates, actually thinking about fit instead of just processing volume."

New High-Value Activities

Practical examples of higher-value work include:

- Running intake discussions with hiring managers that translate business needs into clear, AI-friendly role definitions.
- Reviewing AI-generated shortlists to ensure quality and diversity.
- Providing feedback and coaching to hiring managers on interview quality and candidate experience.
- Partnering with HR analytics teams to interpret trends and suggest process improvements.

The study's findings on efficiency and experience show that these activities are where human judgment adds most value, once automation has cleared space in the recruiter's day.

Recruitment as a Career-Shift, not a Role Adjustment

For many recruiters, this transition is not incremental. It is a shift in career identity.

The traditional recruiter was measured on speed and volume. The AI-enabled recruiter is measured on judgment, influence, and system understanding. This changes how careers progress within talent acquisition.

Three shifts define this transition:

1. From executor to advisor - Recruiters move from executing hiring steps to advising hiring managers on talent markets, role definition, and decision quality.
2. From intuition-led to data-informed - Experience still matters, but it is now complemented by data. Recruiters are expected to interpret signals, not just rely on instinct.
3. From process owner to system thinker - Recruiters must understand how different parts of the hiring system interact, including tools, workflows, and candidate experience.

For organisations, recognising this shift is critical. Without it, recruiters are evaluated using outdated metrics while being asked to perform a fundamentally different role.

Managing Fear, Resistance, and Change

Despite the potential benefits, AI adoption often triggers a deeper concern among recruiters: loss of relevance.

The research and broader adoption literature suggest several levers to manage this transition.

Involve Recruiters Early

Recruiters should be involved in:

- Tool selection discussions (requirements, pain points, priorities).
- Designing pilot processes and testing user flows.

- Providing feedback during configuration and early rollout.

Involving them early turns them from **subjects** of change into **co-creators**.

Train for Understanding, Not Just Usage

Training should go beyond "click paths" to include:

- Why the organisation is using AI and what benefits are expected.
- How the underlying logic works in simple terms (e.g., "The tool matches skills from CVs to the job description and ranks candidates; here's what it ignores").
- When to **trust** the tool and when to **challenge** it.

This builds confidence and reduces the sense that AI is a mysterious black box. It also signals that the organisation is investing in recruiter capability, not just deploying tools.

Celebrate New Wins

Leaders can reinforce the new role by:

- Recognising recruiters who use data to improve sourcing strategies or reduce drop-offs.
- Highlighting examples where a recruiter's judgment caught an issue the AI missed, or where they used AI insights to spot a great candidate.
- Updating performance metrics to reflect advisory and strategic contributions, not just volume of closures.

This makes it clear that the organisation values **augmented** recruiters, not just faster ones.

Metrics That Matter for AI-Powered Recruiters

To support this role shift, organisations must align recruiter metrics with efficiency, experience, and fairness outcomes.

Efficiency Metrics

- Average time-to-hire by role family, adjusted for AI adoption levels.
- Conversion rates at each stage of the funnel.
- Reduction in manual screening time or touchpoints.

Experience Metrics

- Candidate satisfaction or NPS measures at key stages.
- Response time to candidate queries.
- Qualitative feedback from candidates and hiring managers.

Fairness-Related Metrics

- Participation in fairness audits (e.g., providing contextual insights, helping interpret patterns).
- Flagging and escalation of potential bias cases.

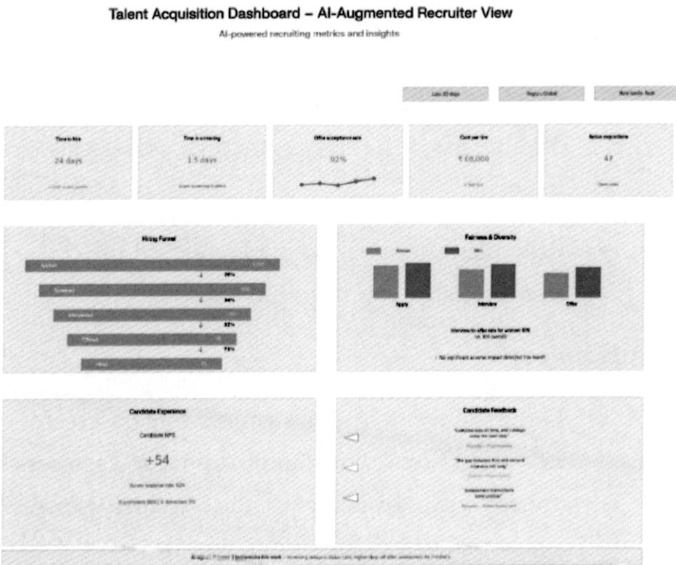

By making these metrics visible and meaningful, organisations reinforce the behaviours that make AI-enabled recruitment both effective and responsible.

Building a Development Path for TA Teams

Finally, leaders should think about TA capability building as a **multi-year journey**, not a one-off training.

A simple development path could look like this:

1. **Foundation:**
    - Introductory sessions on AI in recruitment, study findings, and ethical principles.

- Tool walkthroughs focused on practical usage and common scenarios.

2.Intermediate:

- Workshops on data literacy, reading dashboards, interpreting metrics, and spotting issues.
- Role-play exercises on explaining AI processes to candidates and hiring managers.

3.Advanced:

- Design labs where senior recruiters co-create new workflows, communications, and fairness checks with HR analytics and product teams.
- Opportunities to specialise (e.g., TA analytics, candidate experience design, employer branding).

This turns AI from a threat into a career accelerant for recruiters who lean into the change. Recruitment is transforming into a specialized and forward-thinking function, transcending its traditional role as merely an operational task. This evolution highlights the importance of strategic recruitment in shaping the future of organizations.

From Recruiters to Strategic Talent Partners

As shown in Chapters 3 and 4, AI can deliver strong efficiency gains and support better candidate experiences, but only when human judgment remains central. Recruiters are that human centre. Their role is not shrinking; it is evolving.

In earlier chapters, we focused on **what** AI can do and **how** to design fair, transparent systems. This chapter has argued that **who** operates those systems is just as important. An AI-powered recruiter:

- Understands how AI tools work and where they can fail.
- Uses data to improve hiring decisions and processes.
- Protects fairness and candidate trust through judgment and communication.
- Acts as a bridge between business needs, technology, and candidate expectations.

In **Chapter 7,** we will step fully into the candidate's shoes and design the digital-first, human-centred journeys that your newly empowered recruiters will deliver, closing the loop between efficiency, fairness, and experience.

7

Designing a Candidate Experience That Works in an AI World

The research behind this book shows a clear pattern: professionals celebrate AI for speed and efficiency, while candidates judge recruitment systems primarily on responsiveness, clarity, and perceived fairness. Candidate experience improves significantly when AI-driven processes are paired with strong communication and transparent expectations; without that, even sophisticated tools feel cold and opaque.

This chapter puts the candidate at the centre. It unpacks what candidates told us, walks through a digital-first journey design, and shows how to use AI to enhance, not erode, the human experience of applying, interviewing, and deciding.

What Candidates Told Us

The candidate portion of the study surfaced several important themes.

Trust and Transparency

Candidates reported **higher levels of trust and satisfaction** when recruitment systems offered:

- Prompt acknowledgements of applications.
- Clear explanations of the steps involved.
- Regular updates on status and timelines.

Where these were missing, candidates felt lost, even if the underlying process was faster than traditional methods.

As one candidate put it, "I finished the test and then heard nothing for three weeks. I didn't know if I was rejected or still in the process."

Communication as the Experience Lever

Statistical analysis demonstrated that **communication quality mediates the relationship between technology usage and candidate experience** (mediation coefficient 0.48, $p < 0.05$).

This means:

- AI by itself does not guarantee a good experience.
- When communication is strong, AI-enabled processes are more likely to be perceived as fair and efficient.
- When communication is weak, candidates may resent automation and feel dehumanized.

A candidate described the same kind of experience: "It felt like I was talking to a system, not a company. I had no idea what was happening or who was making decisions."

Perceived Fairness

Most candidates in the study expressed a **generally positive view** of AI fairness. They appreciated structured processes and saw potential for reducing arbitrary human bias. At the same time, they wanted assurance that:

- AI was monitored for bias.
- Humans were still involved in key decisions.
- They would not be rejected by a "black box" without explanation.

These expectations shape how we need to design candidate journeys in AI-enabled environments.

Mapping the Digital-First Candidate Journey

To improve candidate experience, you must first **see the journey the way candidates do**. For a typical IT or ITeS candidate, the journey includes:

1. Discovering the opportunity
2. Considering whether to apply
3. Applying and initial screening
4. Assessments and interviews
5. Decision and offer (or rejection)
6. Pre-joining and transition

At each stage, we will highlight the role of AI, critical human touchpoints, and design choices that matter most.

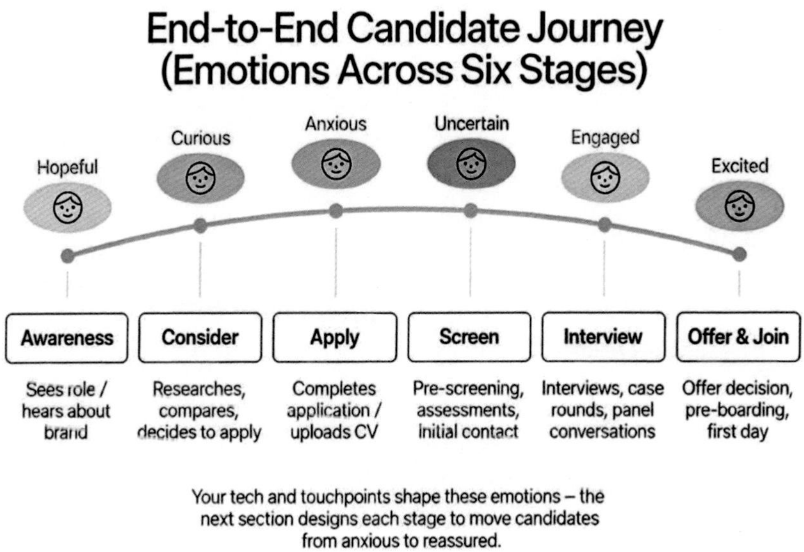

Stage 1 – Discover: "Is this worth my time?"

Candidate questions:

- Who is this company, really?
- Is this role aligned with my skills and aspirations?
- Is this process going to be respectful or a time sink?

AI's role:

- Personalized job recommendations on portals and platforms.

- Targeted ads that reach candidates based on skills and behaviour.

Design actions:

- Ensure job descriptions are specific, honest, and free from jargon that excludes non-traditional backgrounds.
- Provide a simple overview of your AI-enabled recruitment process on the careers site, so candidates know what to expect.
- Show real employee stories, especially in high-demand skill areas, to build credibility.

Stage 2 – Decide to Apply: "Do I trust this process?"

Candidate questions:

- Will my application actually be seen?
- Will I just be filtered out by a machine?
- How long will this take?

This uncertainty shows up clearly in candidate reactions that sound like, "I always wonder if anyone actually reads my profile or if I'm just filtered out before that."

AI's role:

- AI parsers read CVs and populate fields.
- Eligibility checks and basic matching may run even before submission.

Design actions:

- Acknowledge immediately: send a confirmation that clearly states the next steps and approximate timelines.
- Briefly explain how AI will be used in screening (e.g., "We use AI to match your skills with role requirements; recruiters then review the AI shortlist").
- Avoid overly long, repetitive forms when you already have a CV. The more friction you add, the more it feels like a one-way extraction of effort.

Stage 3 – Screening: "Am I being evaluated fairly?"

Candidate questions:

- Did anyone actually look at my profile?
- Was I rejected for a good reason?
- If I were shortlisted, why?

AI's role:

- Resume parsing, skill extraction, and scoring against job criteria.
- Automated filters for non-negotiables (location, legal requirements, critical certifications).

Design actions:

- Communicate outcomes quickly:
- If shortlisted, tell candidates which factors aligned with the role and what the next step is.

- If not shortlisted, send a timely, respectful rejection rather than prolonged silence.
- Where feasible, provide basic feedback categories (e.g., "Skills do not match current role requirements") to reduce guesswork.
- Make it clear that AI supports the process but does not make final hiring decisions.

The fact is, silence at this stage is one of the biggest frustrations, which is evident from many candidates saying things like, "Even a rejection is fine. What's frustrating is not hearing anything at all."

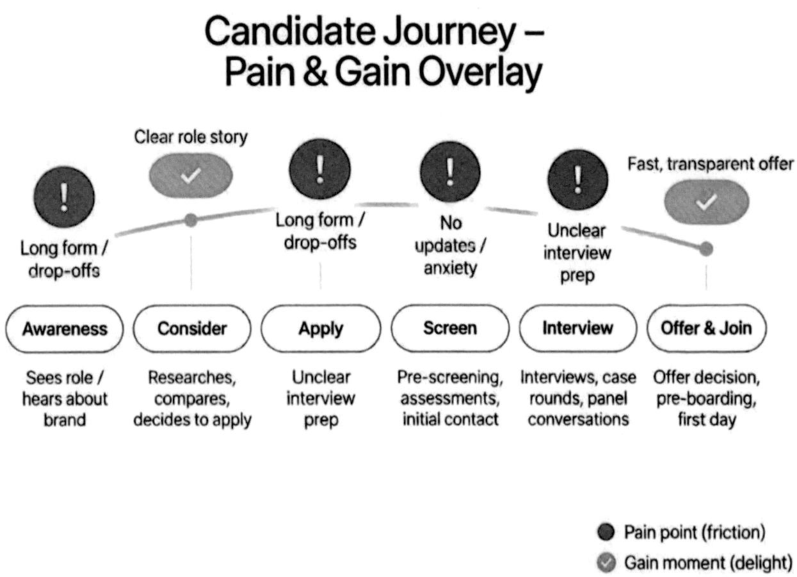

Stage 4 – Assessment and Interviews: "Do they respect my effort?"

Candidate questions:

- How will I be assessed?
- Are the assessments relevant and fair?
- Will I get a chance to tell my story beyond scores?

AI's role:

- Online tests, coding challenges, or simulations.
- Video interviews using structured questions; in some cases, analytics that assist reviewers.
- Automated scheduling and reminders.

Design actions:

- Explain the purpose of each assessment, estimated time, and how results will be used.
- Ensure assessments are job-relevant; avoid generic or excessively long tests that feel disconnected from the role.
- Provide at least minimal feedback where possible (e.g., "You met/exceeded the threshold for X, but fell short on Y").
- Maintain human interactions at key points: a short recruiter call before or after an important stage can dramatically improve perceptions of care.

The research shows that when technology is paired with clear guidance and feedback, candidate satisfaction with AI-enabled recruitment rises noticeably.

Stage 5 – Decision and Offer: "Is this the right move for me?"

Candidate questions:

- Why was I selected or rejected?
- Do I have all the information I need to decide?
- Can I trust this company to treat me fairly after joining?

AI's role:

- Compiling assessment data and feedback for decision-support dashboards.
- Suggesting market-aligned compensation ranges.

Design actions:

- Communicate decisions promptly; long silences between final rounds and offer/rejection harm trust.
- For selected candidates, provide a clear, human-led conversation explaining the offer, role expectations, and growth path.
- For final-stage rejections, consider more personalized feedback, especially in niche IT roles where the candidate invested heavily in the process. At later stages, expectations are even higher. A candidate put it this way - "After four rounds, I expected at least a short explanation. The generic email felt dismissive."

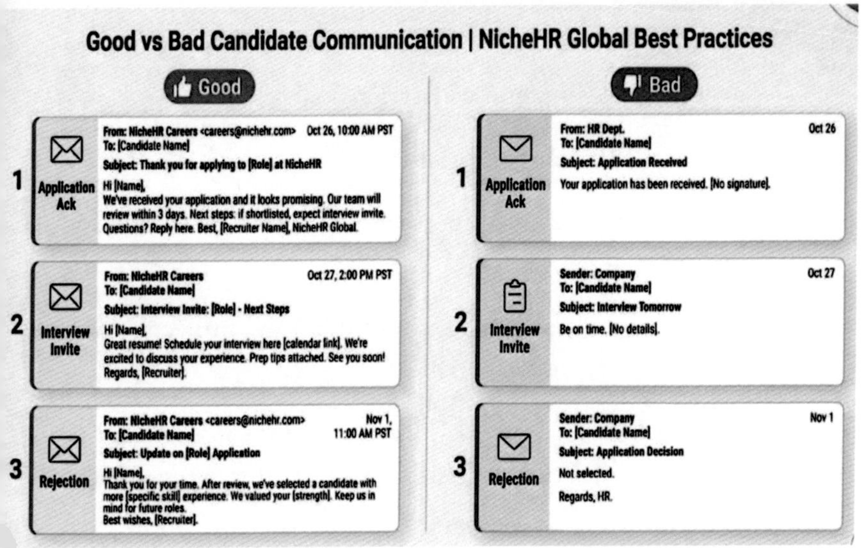

Stage 6 – Pre-Joining: "Are they really invested in me?"

Candidate questions:

- Will they stay in touch until I join?
- Are they serious about integrating me into the team?
- Should I trust them more than my other offers?

AI's role:

- Automated nudges about paperwork, joining logistics, and pre-boarding content.
- Predictive signals indicating potential drop-out risk.

Design actions:

- Blend automation with a personal touch:
- Use AI to manage logistics and reminders.
- Use human calls or messages for critical check-ins and high-value hires.
- Share curated content about the team, projects, and culture to deepen connection.
- Confirm that the same respect and responsiveness shown during hiring will continue after joining.

AI Tools That Actually Enhance Experience

AI can either frustrate or delight. The difference lies in **how** it is implemented.

Chatbots and Virtual Assistants

Used well, chatbots can:

- Answer FAQs 24/7 about process, timelines, and role details.
- Help candidates reschedule interviews without email chains.
- Provide quick links to relevant resources.

They frustrate when:

- They cannot handle common queries and loop candidates endlessly.
- They are positioned as the only way to reach the company.

Status Dashboards and Portals

AI-enabled systems can show real-time status ("application received," "under review," "shortlisted," "on hold"), reducing candidate anxiety.

Design them to:

- Use simple language, not internal codes.
- Update automatically when key changes occur.
- Offer options to withdraw, update details, or ask questions.

Personalization Engines

AI can tailor:

- Recommended roles based on skills and interests.
- Content (blogs, videos, learning resources) aligned with candidate profiles.

When AI Helps vs When It Hurts
(Candidate Experience)

Effective Use of AI ✓	Misuse / Overuse of AI ⚠
Chatbot answers FAQs 24/7 and hands off to a human when questions get complex.	Chatbot blocks access to a human, loops canned replies, and never escalates.
Status dashboard shows real-time application stage and expected next update.	Candidates only receive generic "in process' messages with no dates or clarity.
Personalised nudges: tailored role suggestions and reminders based on profile and consent.	Bulk AI messages feel spammy, creepy, or irrelevant to the candidate.
AI pre-screens to remove obviously unqualified profiles, but recruiters review edge cases.	Black-box auto rejections within minutes, with no human review or appeal path.
Automated surveys collect candidate feedback at key stages, feeding continuous improvement.	No feedback requested; data only used to optimise speed, not experience or fairness.

Used judiciously, this makes candidates feel seen rather than spammed.

Human Moments That Matter Most

Even in a digital-first process, a few **high-impact human interactions** can transform candidate perception:

- **The first live touch:** A short recruiter conversation early in the process can set expectations and answer concerns.
- **Pre-critical stage prep:** A brief call before a major assessment or final interview to clarify format and expectations.

- **Offer discussion:** A thoughtful, two-way conversation about the offer, role, and growth path instead of a one-way email.
- **Gracious closure:** For candidates who reached late stages, a human-delivered rejection with some context.

The study's findings, that candidates value responsiveness and clarity more than raw speed, underline the importance of these touchpoints. A candidate mentioned, "The only time I felt respected was when a recruiter actually called to explain the decision." These moments often define the entire experience.

Measuring and Improving Candidate Experience

To manage candidate experience, you need **data and feedback loops** just as much as you do for efficiency.

Simple Metrics to Track

Inspired by the constructs in the study, you can track:

- **Experience scores** after key stages (short survey questions on clarity, respect, and overall satisfaction).
- **Net Promoter Score (NPS):** "How likely are you to recommend our recruitment process to a friend?"
- **Drop-off points:** Where candidates withdraw or stop responding.
- **Response times:** Average time to acknowledge applications and respond to inquiries.

Closing the Feedback Loop

- Review feedback regularly in TA meetings.
- Identify recurring themes (e.g., confusion after assessments, delays after interviews).
- Test small changes, better templates, added touchpoints, clearer FAQs, and watch whether scores improve.

The same discipline you apply to optimising time-to-hire and cost-per-hire can, and should, be applied to candidate experience.

Candidate Experience Dashboard – Last 90 Days

Tracking key metrics across the recruitment journey

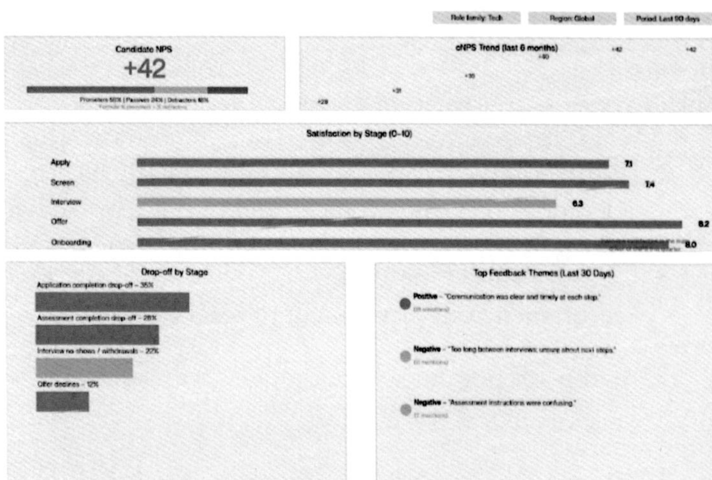

Putting It All Together: The AI-Enabled, Human-Centred Journey

The evidence from your study suggests a simple but powerful design rule:

AI should handle the complexity; humans should own the meaning.

- AI handles volume, pattern recognition, and logistics.
- Human recruiters and hiring managers handle explanation, empathy, and final judgment.

When leaders design journeys against this rule and align them with the communication and fairness insights from earlier chapters, they create recruitment systems that are not only faster and more efficient but also **more trusted**.

In **Chapter 8**, we will zoom out and look at how to scale such systems across entire organisations and regions, with specific playbooks for high-volume ITeS environments, specialist IT hiring, and cross-border expansion into markets like the GCC, turning insights from this book into a 180-day action plan.

8

From Pilot to Scale: Playbooks and a 180-Day Action Plan

By now, the case is clear. AI can improve efficiency and cut costs in IT and ITeS recruitment, especially in high-volume environments. It can coexist with strong candidate experience and perceptions of fairness, provided communication and governance are designed intentionally. The challenge for leaders is no longer *whether* to use AI in talent acquisition, but *how* to move from scattered pilots and tools to a coherent, scalable system.

This chapter offers three things: sector-specific playbooks for IT and ITeS, a simple maturity roadmap, and a practical 180-day action plan for TA and HR leaders who want to act on the evidence in this book.

Why Pilots Succeed, and Scaling Fails

Many organisations report promising results in early AI pilots: faster shortlists, enthusiastic recruiters, and positive internal buzz. Yet, when they attempt to scale these solutions across functions, locations, or role families, they encounter familiar problems:

- Tools that work well in one unit do not integrate cleanly with enterprise systems elsewhere.
- Practices that suit a high-volume ITeS process do not translate neatly to specialised IT hiring.
- Governance and fairness checks that were optional in pilots become critical under broader use.

The research shows that AI's impact varies by sector and context. ITeS organisations in the study saw **stronger improvements** in time-to-hire and cost-per-hire than IT firms, reflecting their more standardized, volume-driven hiring needs. IT roles, by contrast, often require more nuanced evaluation and human judgment.

Scaling requires acknowledging these differences and designing **sector-appropriate playbooks** rather than forcing a single model on the whole enterprise.

Playbook A – Scaling AI in High-Volume ITeS Hiring

Large ITeS providers and shared service centres handle thousands of similar roles each year, including customer support, back-office processing, and other operations functions. Here, the efficiency benefits of AI are most pronounced.

Design Priorities

- **Maximise automation where rules are clear.** Use AI extensively in sourcing, screening, and assessments for standardised roles, supported by clear eligibility and performance criteria.

- **Standardise processes across locations.**
  Consistency enables better measurement, fairness checks, and continuous improvement.

- **Guard fairness using routine audits.**
  Because volume is high, even small biases can affect large numbers of candidates. Regular fairness reviews by gender, location, and institution become essential.

Key Elements of the ITeS Playbook

1. **Unified AI-Enabled Funnel**

   - Single ATS integrating sourcing, AI screening, assessments, and communications.

   - Pre-defined, AI-readable role templates for major role families.

2. **Automation Highlights**

   - Resume parsing and matching as default.

   - Online assessments for language, aptitude, and job-specific skills.

   - Automated communication at key touchpoints, with human contact for late-stage candidates.

3. **Governance Practices**

   - Quarterly fairness audits of shortlist and assessment outcomes across key demographic groups.

   - Recruiter review of a sample of auto-rejected applications each cycle.

4. **Candidate Experience Enhancers**

    - Clear "What to Expect in Our Process" guide shared early.
    - Mobile-friendly status tracking and FAQs.
    - Opt-in feedback surveys after assessment and final decisions.

ITeS AI Hiring Playbook – One-Page Canvas

Context • High-volume support roles • Shift work, SLA-driven • Global English plus local language needs	**AI Role** • Bulk sourcing & screening • Traffic shaping to right queues • Chatbots for FAQs & scheduling
Human Role • Final shortlisting and offers • Coaching candidates on roles Handling exceptions & escalations	**Key Risks** • Over-automation and depersonalisation • Bias in language and accent filtering Handling sensitive customer data

When executed well, this playbook aligns closely with the study's findings: high automation in screening and assessment delivers significant efficiency gains, while structured communication and fairness monitoring maintain trust.

Playbook B – Scaling AI in Specialist IT Hiring

IT organisations and tech divisions of larger companies often focus on smaller volumes of harder-to-fill roles, such as architects, senior developers, data scientists, and product managers. Here, the cost of a mis-hire is high, and nuanced, context-based judgment matters more.

Design Priorities

- **Use AI to augment, not replace, human judgment.** Focus on sourcing, information consolidation, and logistics rather than fully automated decisions.

- **Preserve human-led evaluation.**
  Ensure technical and behavioural interviews remain central to decision-making.
- **Elevate experience for critical talent.**
  Design journeys that feel personal, even when AI is supporting the backend.

Key Elements of the IT Playbook

1. **Targeted AI Sourcing**
    - Use AI to discover candidates with specific skill combinations across platforms and internal databases.
    - Enable recruiters to build and manage micro-talent pools (for example, cloud security specialists or data engineers in a particular metro).
2. **Structured Screening with Human Oversight**
    - Resume parsing for better comparability, but minimal auto-rejection at early stages.
    - Recruiters review most profiles surfaced by AI, applying contextual knowledge.
3. **Advanced Scheduling and Coordination**
    - Use AI scheduling assistants to reduce back-and-forth across busy calendars.
    - Automate reminders and logistics without over-automating the conversations themselves.

4. **Premium Candidate Experience**

    - Early recruiter conversations to understand career goals and constraints.
    - Clear communication about how assessment results feed into decisions.
    - Personalised closure and feedback for late-stage candidates.

IT AI Hiring Playbook – One-Page Canvas

Context	**AI Role**
• Specialist engineering and product roles • Competitive talent markets • Hybrid and remote teams	• Targeted sourcing in niche communities • Technical screening assistance • Market and compensation insights
Human Role • Deep role discovery with hiring managers • Portfolio and culture-add assessment • Closing and counteroffer handling	**Key Risks** • Over-reliance on keyword matching • Screening out non-traditional talent • Opacity of complex models

Key Metrics
- Time to fill & cost per hire
- First-90-day performance & attrition
  Candidate NPS and fairness indicators
- Quality of hire proxies
- (ramp-up, code quality)
- Hiring manager satisfaction
- Diversity of slate and hires

In this playbook, AI is a **force multiplier**, not an arbiter; it helps recruiters and hiring managers see more, faster, but does not decide on their behalf.

A Four-Stage Maturity Roadmap

To move from ad-hoc use of tools to strategic, governed AI in TA, organisations can follow a simple maturity model.

Stage 1 – Digitised Hiring

Characteristics:

- Basic ATS in place; job postings and applications are digital.

- Limited analytics; data mostly used retrospectively.

Risks:

- Manual screening and coordination still dominate the recruiter workload.
- Candidate experience and fairness are highly dependent on individual recruiters.

Stage 2 – Assisted AI

Characteristics:

- AI features implemented for screening, chatbots, or scheduling in parts of the funnel.
- Recruiters still heavily involved in decision-making but supported by tools.

Risks:

- Fragmentation: different teams using different tools with little integration.
- Limited governance; fairness and transparency mostly implicit.

Stage 3 – Integrated AI with Governance

Characteristics:

- AI tools integrated into a coherent end-to-end process, aligned with clear design principles.
- Standardised communication templates and status visibility for candidates.

- Regular fairness audits and clear ownership of AI configuration and monitoring.

Benefits:

- Strong, measurable gains in efficiency and cost; improved candidate experience and stable perceptions of fairness.

Stage 4 – Continuous Learning and Innovation

Characteristics:

- TA teams use data to continuously refine criteria, communications, and process flows.
- New AI capabilities are piloted in a controlled way, with clear success metrics and rollback plans.
- Candidates and hiring managers are involved in feedback loops for ongoing improvement.

Benefits:

- AI in TA becomes a strategic capability, not just a set of tools, buttressed by evidence and trusted by stakeholders

AI-in-TA Maturity Ladder – From Experiments to Operating Model

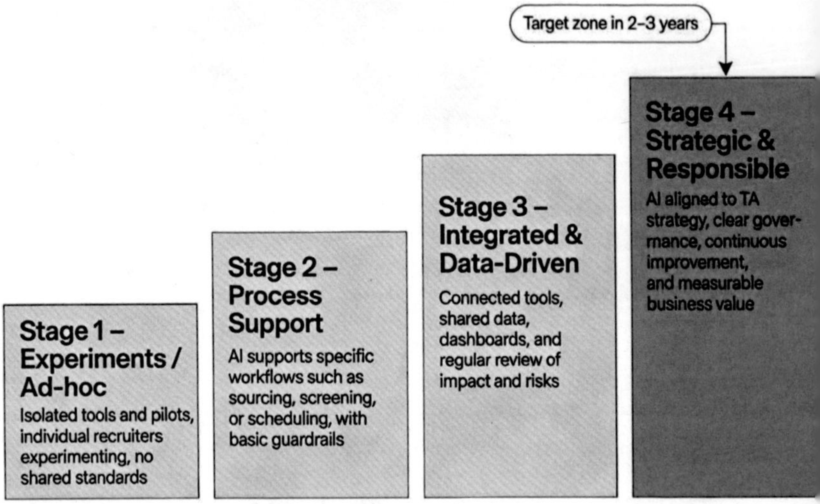

The empirical findings in your research, particularly around the relationships between AI, efficiency, communication, experience, and fairness, offer clear guardrails at each stage of this roadmap.

Scaling Across Geographies: India to GCC and Beyond

Many Indian IT and ITeS firms also recruit for roles in the GCC and other regions. While the core principles of AI-enabled, human-centred TA travel well, three factors require local adaptation:

- **Regulation and compliance** – Data privacy, AI use, and anti-discrimination laws vary by country and may impose specific restrictions or obligations.

- **Cultural expectations** – Communication styles, interview norms, and candidate expectations around feedback can differ significantly.
- **Market dynamics** – Availability of skills, competition, and employer brand positioning may demand different sourcing and engagement strategies.

The framework in this book is flexible enough to extend to other markets: AI handles volume and pattern recognition; humans handle context, fairness, and relationship management. What changes from one geography to another is **how you tune the model**, not the underlying logic.

A 180-Day Action Plan for Leaders

To help you turn insight into action, here is a pragmatic six-month roadmap for CHROs, TA heads, and business leaders in IT and ITeS.

Days 1–30: Diagnose and Align

- **Map the current funnel** end-to-end for major role families (e.g., ITeS operations, IT development, leadership roles). Mark where AI is used, where humans decide, and where communication happens.
- **Collect baseline metrics** for time-to-hire, cost-per-hire, candidate experience (if available), and basic fairness indicators (e.g., gender ratios at each stage).
- **Align leadership** on the design principles: automate volume, design around communication, make fairness a feature, and keep humans in the loop.

Days 31–90: Design and Pilot

- **Select 1–2 pilot areas**:
  - A high-volume ITeS role family.
  - A critical specialist IT role family.
- **Redesign the funnel** for each pilot following Chapter 4's stage-by-stage guidance, explicitly specifying:
  - AI tasks vs human tasks.
  - Communication at each candidate touchpoint.
  - Fairness checks and escalation paths.
- **Train recruiters and hiring managers** in the pilot areas on:
  - How the tools work.
  - How to interpret outputs.
  - How to communicate about AI with candidates.
- **Run the pilots** for a complete hiring cycle, capturing data on efficiency, experience, and fairness.

Days 91–135: Evaluate and Refine

- **Compare pilot metrics** to baseline:
  - Time-to-hire and cost-per-hire.
  - Candidate satisfaction or NPS for those roles.
  - Fairness indicators across key groups.

- **Gather qualitative feedback** from recruiters, hiring managers, and candidates.
- **Refine processes** where you see friction or risk, communications, thresholds, and human review stages.

This is where you move from "what we expect based on the thesis" to "what we see in our environment," tuning the system to your culture and constraints.

Days 136–180: Scale and Institutionalize

- **Extend redesigned funnels** to additional role families that resemble the pilots.
- **Formalize governance** by:
- Documenting your AI in recruitment policy.
- Assigning clear roles for monitoring and configuration.
- Scheduling regular fairness and performance reviews.
- **Roll out capability-building** for the broader TA team:
- Tool training.
- Data literacy basics.
- Workshops on candidate communication and fairness awareness.
- **Communicate your story** internally and, where appropriate, externally:
- Why you are using AI.
- How you protect fairness and candidate experience.

- How this strengthens the organisation's ability to attract and grow talent.

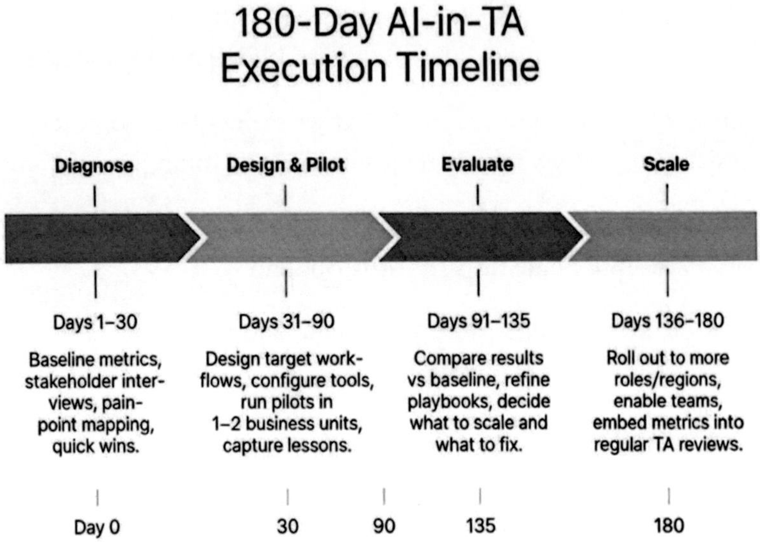

Closing the Loop, and Looking Ahead

This book began with a simple tension: AI promises to transform hiring, but its real impact, especially in a complex market like Indian IT and ITeS, has often been uneven in practice.

The evidence showed that AI can improve efficiency and reduce cost, particularly through structured automation in screening and shortlisting. It also showed that candidate experience improves only when technology is supported by strong communication and visible fairness.

Across the chapters, those insights were translated into action:

- A clear architecture for an AI-first, human-centred hiring funnel.
- Practical frameworks for fairness, transparency, and governance.
- A redefined role for recruiters as AI-powered talent partners.
- Guidance on designing candidate experiences that work in a digital-first environment.
- Playbooks and a structured path to move from pilots to scaled, governed implementation.

What this chapter has shown is how to bring all of these elements together, not as isolated initiatives, but as a coherent system that can be implemented, measured, and improved over time.

But implementation is only one part of the story.

The next question is what happens as these systems mature. As AI becomes more embedded in hiring, how will regulation evolve? How will roles continue to change? What new capabilities will become essential? And what will define leadership in this space over the next few years?

The final chapter looks ahead to those questions. It brings together the themes of this book and explores how AI and human judgment will continue to shape the future of hiring.

9

The Future of AI and Human Hiring

This book has explored a single idea from multiple angles: that AI is reshaping recruitment, but its value depends entirely on how it is used.

We began by understanding why hiring has become a strategic constraint in Indian IT and ITeS. We then examined why many AI-enabled initiatives fail to deliver, not because the technology is weak, but because it is layered onto broken or incomplete systems. The research showed where AI creates real value, in efficiency, speed, and consistency, and where it does not, particularly in candidate experience and fairness without strong communication and governance.

From there, the focus shifted to design. How to build an AI-first, human-centred hiring funnel. How to operationalise fairness. How to redefine the recruiter's role. How to design candidate journeys that are both digital and human. And finally, how to scale these practices across organisations in a structured, disciplined way.

Taken together, these are not isolated improvements. They describe a shift in how hiring itself is understood, from a process to be managed to a system to be designed.

The future of hiring builds on that shift.

From Systems to Ecosystems

The first phase of AI in recruitment was about tools. The second phase, which many organisations are still navigating, is about systems. The next phase will be about ecosystems.

Hiring will increasingly operate across interconnected layers, internal platforms, external talent marketplaces, assessment ecosystems, and learning systems that feed back into hiring decisions. The question will no longer be which tool to deploy, but how these components work together.

Organisations that treat hiring as an integrated ecosystem will have a structural advantage over those that continue to optimise individual steps in isolation.

AI Agents and Assisted Decision-Making

AI in recruitment is also moving toward greater autonomy. Systems are beginning to do more than assist; they are starting to act.

AI agents can already support sourcing, candidate engagement, scheduling, and early-stage evaluation with minimal intervention. Over time, their role will expand.

This does not remove the need for human involvement. It sharpens it.

The critical decisions shift from execution to control:

- **Where should AI act independently?**
- **Where must human judgment intervene?**
- **How are decisions reviewed, explained, and challenged?**

The organisations that answer these questions clearly will be able to use automation without losing accountability.

The Shift to Skills-Based Hiring

One of the most important structural changes ahead is the move toward skills-based hiring.

AI makes it possible to assess candidates more directly, through structured evaluations, simulations, and demonstrated capability rather than relying only on degrees or past titles.

This expands access to talent, but it also raises the bar for design.

Poorly designed assessments can exclude just as easily as outdated filters. Well-designed ones can open pathways that did not exist before.

In that sense, skills-based hiring is not just an efficiency improvement. It is a shift in how opportunity is distributed.

The Recruiter as Strategist

As automation becomes more embedded, the recruiter's role continues to evolve.

Earlier chapters described the move from transactional work to advisory capability. The next step is strategic ownership.

Recruiters will increasingly:

- Shape hiring strategy, not just execute it.
- Interpret talent market signals and guide decision-making.

- Influence how AI is configured and used within the organisation.
- Act as custodians of candidate experience and fairness.

This makes capability building central. AI literacy, data interpretation, communication, and ethical judgment become defining skills for the function.

Recruitment, in this model, is no longer operational support. It is a strategic capability.

Regulation and Accountability

As AI becomes more central to hiring decisions, regulatory attention is increasing.

Across markets, there is a clear direction toward greater transparency, stronger fairness requirements, and clearer accountability for algorithm-influenced decisions.

For organisations, this means:

- Decisions must be explainable, not just efficient.
- Processes must be auditable, not just scalable.
- Responsibilities must be defined, not assumed.

What may feel like compliance pressure is, in practice, a push toward maturity. It forces hiring systems to become more disciplined and more defensible.

Ethical AI as a Differentiator

Ethics in hiring is often framed as risk avoidance. Avoid bias. Avoid complaints. Avoid regulatory issues.

But there is another side to it.

Candidates are increasingly sensitive to how they are treated. Transparency, clarity, and fairness are not abstract principles. They shape perception and trust.

Organisations that demonstrate these consistently will stand out.

Ethical AI, when implemented well, becomes a differentiator. It signals seriousness, credibility, and respect for candidates.

What Will Not Change

For all the change ahead, some fundamentals remain constant.

Hiring is still about making decisions under uncertainty. Candidates are still evaluating organisations as much as they are being evaluated. Trust is still built through clarity, responsiveness, and respect.

AI changes how these are delivered. It does not remove their importance.

In fact, as automation increases, the human moments in the process become more visible and more important.

A Final Perspective

The core message of this book is clear and powerful: AI-enabled recruitment isn't just a shortcut or a replacement, it's an amplifier.

It enhances effective systems and uncovers flaws in poorly designed ones. While it accelerates processes, it also magnifies the impact of weak decisions. It holds the potential to promote fairness, but only if we intentionally design and monitor for it.

The future of hiring won't hinge on the extent of AI adoption but on the wisdom of its integration with human judgment.

In a dynamic world where change is the only constant, the most effective leaders will be those who go beyond the superficial. They will create robust systems that stand the test of time rather than simply implementing quick-fix tools. True leadership lies in the commitment to cultivating talent and fostering enduring capabilities instead of just acquiring the latest technologies. Moreover, these leaders will understand the vital importance of balancing efficiency with user experience, ensuring that the pursuit of speed does not compromise fairness or inclusivity. This holistic approach will define their success in transforming challenges into opportunities.

The path forward is unmistakable. The tools are at our disposal, and evidence of their impact is already emerging.

What remains is a decisive commitment to act with purpose. This intentionality will define the future of hiring.

Verses Kindler Publication

Verses Kindler Publication

Reach us through our website -

https://www.verseskindlerpublication.com/

For more information visit our

Instagram or Facebook page.

For more information visit our

Instagram or Facebook page